The Best
Stage Scenes
# of 2002

Smith and Kraus *Books for Actors*

YOUNG ACTOR SERIES

Great Scenes and Monologues for Children Volumes I and II

Forensics Series Volume I: Duo Practice and Competition: Thirty-five
8–10 Minute Original Comedic Plays

Forensics Series Volume II: Duo Practice and Competition: Thirty-five
8–10 Minute Original Dramatic Plays

Great Scenesin Dialect for Young Actors Volumes I and II

Great Scenes for Young Actors Volumes I and II

Short Scenes and Monologues for Middle School Actors

Multicultural Scenes for Young Actors

SCENE STUDY SERIES

The Best Stage Scenes of 2001

The Best Stage Scenes of 2000

The Best Stage Scenes of 1999

The Best Stage Scenes of 1998

The Best Stage Scenes of 1997

The Best Stage Scenes of 1996

The Best Stage Scenes of 1995

The Best Stage Scenes of 1994

The Best Stage Scenes of 1993

The Best Stage Scenes of 1992

The Best Stage Scenes for Men from the 1980s

The Best Stage Scenes for Women from the 1980s

The Ultimate Scene Study Series Volume I: 101 Short Scenes for Groups

The Ultimate Scene Study Series Volume II: 102 Short Scenes for Two Actors

The Ultimate Scene Study Series Volume III: 103 Short Scenes for Three Actors

The Ultimate Scene Study Series Volume IV: 104 Short Scenes for Four Actors

Kiss and Tell—Restoration Comedy of Manners: Scenes, Monologues, and
Historical Context

A Brave and Violent Theatre Monologues, Scenes and Historical Context for
20th Century Irish Drama

Scenes from Classic Plays 468 BC to 1970 AD

If you require prepublication information about upcoming Smith and Kraus books,
you may receive our semiannual catalogue, free of charge, by sending your name
and address to *Smith and Kraus Catalogue, PO Box 127, Lyme, NH 03768. Or call
us at (800) 895-4331; fax: (603) 643-6431.*

The Best
Stage Scenes
of 2002

edited by D. L. Lepidus

SCENE STUDY SERIES

A SMITH AND KRAUS BOOK

Published by Smith and Kraus, Inc.
177 Lyme Road, Hanover, NH 03755
www.SmithKraus.com

First Edition: November 2003
10 9 8 7 6 5 4 3 2 1

Cover illustration by Lisa Goldfinger
Cover and text design by Julia Hill Gignoux

The Scene Study Series 1067-3253
ISBN 1-57525-328-3

NOTE: These scenes are intended to be used for audition and class study; permission is not required to use the material for those purposes. However, if there is a paid performance of any of the scenes included in this book, please refer to the permissions acknowledgment pages 223–231 to locate the source that can grant permission for public performance.

Contents

Scenes for Two Women

Scenes for Two Men

Foreword

Every year, I read or see hundreds of new plays. The scenes in this book are the best ones I could find from plays produced or published in 2002. The question you may well ask is what do I mean by "best"? What were my criteria in selecting these scenes?

First and foremost, I looked for scenes that would be useful to the people who buy these scene books: actors and acting students, most of whom are under fifty (indeed, under forty; indeed, under thirty). Actors, in general, want to work on material, either for class use or for auditions, which is age-appropriate to themselves.

Also, I wanted to provide a wide range of characters and dramatic situations, from the comic to the not-so-comic, in scenes with an interesting dramatic action, preferably one with some conflict. These are, certainly, the most useful to you, whether in class or for that important audition or "scene night" showcase.

Finally, I tried to provide a nice mixture of scenes by well-known playwrights with the work of those less well-known. So, you will find herein excellent scenes from new plays by the likes of John Patrick Shanley, Marsha Norman, Athol Fugard, A.R. Gurney, and Craig Lucas; but you will find wonderful scenes as well from fine, up-and-coming playwrights like Kelly McAllister, Gina Gionfriddo, Donna Spector, Christopher Shinn, Don Nigro, and Jessica Goldberg, to name but a few of the many fine writers who have allowed me to include their work in this volume.

Oh, and one other thing: Every single one of these scenes is from a published play, readily available either in an acting edition or trade anthology. (See the Permissions section in the back of this book for publisher information.) Because if you're working on a scene, you need to be able to read the whole play, don't you?

Once again: My thanks to Marisa Smith and Eric Kraus for entrusting this anthology to me. It's a lot of work, but when I think of all you actors benefiting from it, in your classes and in your auditions, it's definitely worth the effort.

D. L. Lepidus

Scenes for
One Man and
One Woman

A.M. **Sunday**
Jerome Hairston

Helen and R.P. are a mixed-race couple in their late thirties. She's white; he's black. She has recently learned about Another Woman. She is leaving him.

Thursday morning. Lights on Helen. She is dressed well. She carries a wrapped box in one hand, a ribbon in the other. She places the box on the table. She begins delicately garnishing the box with the ribbon, taking the proper time to get it right. Eventually she feels the presence of R.P.

HELEN: Early.

R.P.: Denny's coughin'.

HELEN: Is he?

R.P.: Runnin' around bare feet. Got him coughin', I guess.

HELEN: Mmmn.

(Silence.)

R.P.: You look nice.

HELEN: Thank you.

R.P.: That the reason?

HELEN: For?

R.P.: Why you left bed so early.

HELEN: I took some time to straighten the place up a bit. Sometimes a mess don't announce itself until there's the prospect of company. Funny how that happens.

R.P.: You really thing he's going to ask her?

HELEN: Better safe than sorry, I suppose. Either way, it had me *into* things. I was rummaging.

R.P.: I know. I heard you. Makin' these . . . small rackets.

HELEN: Well, it only filled three-quarters. The pictures. The box they were in. Used to be full. And I checked. Looked for pieces, flakes of film or something. Thinkin' maybe they've corroded, wasted away. That time wasted . . . They go for so long unchecked. And in dark places maybe they just start fading. But I didn't see anything like that. No trace of something there that's going, just gone. Less than before, I find it strange. So, I had to take the time to find something more suitable. Bringing me here. To this box here. *(Pause.)* So, I wake you?

R.P.: Just said. Denny's coughing.

HELEN: That's right. You did. You said.

R.P.: Hacking something fierce. Figured I'd go ahead and face the inevitable.

HELEN: The inevitable?

R.P.: He's not going anywhere. School. Not with that sort of noise comin' from him. No. He's stayin' home.

HELEN: Maybe you should wait. Maybe it'll pass.

R.P.: Don't think so. All night I been in tune. Kept me up anticipatin'. Anticipatin' this morning. The mess when he wakes. Anticipatin' Denny the wakin' mess.

(Silence.)

R.P.: How many you think?

HELEN: What?

R.P.: You're suggestin' it's small, but it seems an awful lot. The box I'm saying.

HELEN: What about it?

R.P.: A good amount there. Pictures. Moments.

HELEN: I suppose.

R.P.: How many years' worth?

HELEN: Sixteen. Seventeen maybe.

R.P.: And you're taking the day. Just one day.

HELEN: Yes. One day.

R.P.: Even if you took the week. The month. The year. You think it'd be enough?

HELEN: Enough?

R.P.: To sit her down. One by one. And tell her. What each one means. Give her the proper understanding. Of what she's seeing. Who she's seeing. Why certain days. Or nights. Or whatever. Why they seemed worthy. To hold on to. To be reminded of. I just don't know if you can gift somebody that. Your history. Even if it does got a ribbon.

HELEN: Yeah. Well, it's tied so. So, it looks like I'm committed.

R.P.: Are you staying?

HELEN: I didn't go through all this trouble just to stand here.

R.P.: I'm sayin'. If she lets you in. You plan on stayin'?

HELEN: It's why I'm going isn't it?

R.P.: Stayin' for real. For a while.

HELEN: Why?

R.P.: I think you should. Stay, I mean.

HELEN: What would keep me?

R.P.: If that's your gift. Then you should take the time. However long. To make her realize what she's been given. 'Cause it's such a long way, Helen. Just to end up feeling . . . foolish.

HELEN: Check Denny's forehead. Check it frequently. He fevers so easily.

R.P.: Just something you should think about.

HELEN: Make sure to see Jay off. He loves to oversleep.

R.P.: Did you hear me?

HELEN: Three to four hour trip. I'll have plenty of time. To think.

R.P.: No need to call. If the day ends. You're not here. I'll know.

HELEN: Fine.

R.P.: What now?

HELEN: I leave. *(Pause.)* Are you going to say good-bye? *(Nothing.)* Or have you been saying good-bye?

R.P.: I don't think so.

HELEN: Then what would you call it?

R.P.: Sayin' hello to something else.

(They look at one another. Helen exits.)

A.M. **Sunday**
Jerome Hairston

Jay and Lorie are teenagers. He's mixed-race; she's white. They are boyfriend/girlfriend, and their relationship is causing problems at school.

Lights up on Jay and Lorie. Same morning. Outside. The woods. Jay stands. Lorie looks to the distance.

LORIE: Three minutes since. Three or four. Since the first bell. In case you didn't hear. And then there's ten, ten I think, minutes between first and late bell. In case you didn't know. And you got to cut back through the gym. Through that alley. That adds time. 'Cause you got to walk careful through there. I know. I've slipped before. In case you were wondering. I mean, if I knew. Knew I was gonna meet you. That out here meant, you know, the woods. I would've prepared myself better. Wouldn't have worn something so . . . delicate.

JAY: What is that anyway?

LORIE: What is what?

JAY: That you're wearing. Is that a skirt? Or they pants?

LORIE: Kind of like both.

JAY: What is it silk or something?

LORIE: I don't know. Some sort of cotton thing.

JAY: So, what do you mean by delicate?

LORIE: This color kind of begs to be dirtied, don't you think?

JAY: Didn't have to come if you didn't want to.

LORIE: What makes you think I didn't want to?

JAY: Your words. They got a tone.

LORIE: Just being out this far. Not exactly the smartest move, you know. Might miss roll.

JAY: If you're so worried, feel free. Just know. You'd be risking it.

LORIE: Risking what?

JAY: Four I've felt. Counted each one. Four in a row. First, it was one every few minutes. But now . . . Somethin's definitely on its way.

LORIE: You're counting raindrops?

JAY: Yeah.

LORIE: So you have a sense? How close? The rain?

JAY: Yeah.

LORIE: Did you know I waited for you last night? From six to seven-thirty. I waited. At the park. Did you know that?

JAY: I did.

LORIE: Did you know you didn't show up?

JAY: I'm aware.

LORIE: Do you want to keep going, or go back to ignoring it?

JAY: I wasn't ignoring it.

LORIE: What would you call it?

JAY: Getting up nerve I guess.

LORIE: For what?

(Pause. He goes into his backpack. He gives her a plastic bag.)

JAY: You should keep it closed.

LORIE: Why?

JAY: There's colors inside. The rain. They'll bleed.

LORIE: What is it?

JAY: It's a gift. For you. You and your hair. *(Pause. Looks up.)* That's five. Five more. Five will turn into six. And keep going.

LORIE: Jay?

JAY: You'll get stuck here. You should go.

LORIE: What about you?

JAY: What about me?

LORIE: You're not coming to school?

JAY: Nope. Staying right here.

LORIE: You'll soak yourself.

JAY: I got cover enough. Besides. Too far to walk home.

(They stand. A moment passes.)

LORIE: I didn't say thank you. For the present.

JAY: You don't got to thank me.

LORIE: But I appreciate it. I do. The thought. You thinking of me like that. But that's not the reason, is it?

JAY: For?

LORIE: The woods. Your voice. Just doesn't sound right to me.

JAY: How does it sound?

LORIE: Unfinished.

JAY: *(Pause.)* Guess there's something else. Something else I was supposed to ask you.

LORIE: Then why don't you?

JAY: 'Cause if I did. You would have to answer. And I don't think you'd want to.

LORIE: You don't know that.

JAY: I'm pretty sure I do.

LORIE: Ask me anyway. And we'll see.

JAY: Alright then. Is it true?

LORIE: Is what true?

JAY: Lorie sucks nigger dick. *(Pause.)* That's what I heard. Lorie sucks nigger dick. Is it true?
   (Pause.)

LORIE: I didn't.

JAY: Didn't what?

LORIE: I didn't expect that.

JAY: I'm standing outside school yesterday. The sun shining. Shining like always. On everything, everywhere. I'm thinking about summer. Your green swoop and ribboned hair. Thinking so deep, I almost don't hear it. But I do. I most definitely hear.

LORIE: Who said it?

JAY: Does it matter?

LORIE: What did you do?

JAY: I got jealous. Angry jealous. On the hunt, wanting to know. Who this guy was. His name. And if he knew, knew about me and you. I mean, really, who the hell this nigger think he is? *(Pause.)* You know, it only took half a second. For the answer to sink in. I've had his name my whole life. But it's like I never even heard it. Till then. Suddenly the sun grows brighter. Hotter, harsher. A half-second later the world's different. That's what happens when a question and an answer come together, I guess. The world changes. It's an amazing thing the first time you realize that. You start listenin' for it to change all the time. *(Pause.)* You do understand my question, right?

LORIE: I believe I do.

JAY: So is it? Is it true?

LORIE: What if I don't answer?

JAY: If you don't answer. That means you don't see me. That you never saw me. Then I'll have no choice. I'll have no choice but to hate you. To hate you deep. And that's not what I want to do. Out here. In the woods. The rain.

LORIE: Jay . . .

JAY: So much gets left unsaid in this world. So much. I need it to change. No matter what it looks like after. So, just tell me. Tell me the truth. Lorie sucks nigger dick. Is it true?

LORIE: Yes.

(Silence.)

JAY: Eleven. I counted eleven that time.

LORIE: I love you.

JAY: Thirteen. Fourteen. You should go.

LORIE: You think you could love me? *(Nothing.)* Jay? *(Nothing.)* Jay, I asked you a question.

JAY: Three o'clock. When the bell rings. I want you to find me. Come find me here.

LORIE: What then?

JAY: We can find somewhere else. Somewhere dark. You and me. In the dark.

LORIE: Then what?

JAY: I'll give you an answer. *(Pause.)* Too many to count now. *(Looking up.)* It's started.

ARMITAGE
Don Nigro

Zachary Pendragon, twenty-six, walks with Eva Trelawny Cornish, twenty, in her father's garden in New York in the year 1804. Zach has just returned from Europe, a trip he made in part to try and forget Eva, with whom he fell in love at a masquerade four years earlier, before he realized she was engaged to James Cornish, his best friend at Yale. Now James and Eva are married, and Zach has come to pay a call on them, but the sexual tension between Zach and Eva is just as strong as ever. Eva loves James, but her attraction to Zach is deeper and more dangerous, and she's still a bit angry at him for running off to Europe. Zach is determined not to betray his friend, but he is still inexorably drawn to Eva. Both know that James could appear at any moment.

Zach and Eva walking in the garden in New York in the year 1804.

ZACH: We're like Adam and Eve here, in your father's garden.

EVA: No we're not

ZACH: I'm speaking metaphorically.

EVA: We'll stop it. I hate that. For one thing, we're completely clothed, although I suppose that could easily be remedied. For another, you are merely an intruder. If I'm to be cast as Eve, my husband must be Adam.

ZACH: Then what does that make me?

EVA: I don't know. Do you swallow rodents?

ZACH: I might if you ask me to.

EVA: I think we'd better go in now. I've grown much too warm.

ZACH: The sun has just gone down.

EVA: It's not the sun I'm speaking of. Could you possibly contrive to stand a little farther away from me?

ZACH: I'm not anywhere near you.

EVA: You're much too close.

ZACH: Where would you like me to stand?

EVA: How about Vermont?

ZACH: I see you haven't lost your sharp tongue.

EVA: I don't recall that you've had much acquaintance with my tongue. You know very little, if anything, about the past or present condition of my tongue or any of my other internal organs, for that matter, if the tongue can be properly considered an internal organ, which I supposed it must be, unless one is sticking it out, which I only do on special occasions. Do not touch me.

ZACH: I'm not touching you.

EVA: Well, something is.

ZACH: Perhaps my relative proximity has set off a particularly vivid set of recollections.

EVA: No, I have no recollections. I disapprove of them. I'm presently abstaining from all manner of remembrance.

ZACH: You don't remember the masquerade party?

EVA: Especially not that.

ZACH: There is a special place in Hell reserved for liars and beautiful women. I hope to go there when I die.

EVA: I'm sure you will. In any case, I was, after all, merely a child.

ZACH: At the masquerade party.

EVA: Yes.

ZACH: The one you can't remember.

EVA: That's the one.

ZACH: But it was only four years ago.

EVA: Four years and thirty-six days.

ZACH: Thirty-five.

EVA: I believe that in your computation you've failed to take into account the second leap year. Besides, I was not a married woman then. I was only sixteen. I've since born two. I think two, yes, two daughters. I'm twenty now. Old age has begun debilitate me. I can feel my soul beginning to blister and crack under the strain of gravity and dinner parties. God is sunburning my brain. If you dare step so much as one centimeter closer to me I shall call out the local constabulary. I shriek extremely forcefully. I practice in my sleep and occasionally during sexual congress. I'm going in now.

ZACH: You don't want to go in.

EVA: I don't see what that's got to do with it.

ZACH: You should have stayed longer at the masquerade.

EVA: If I'd stayed longer, you would have undoubtedly have succeeded in penetrating my disguise. In any case it was you who left first.

ZACH: No you left first.

EVA: I'm not going to argue about events which I refuse on principle to recollect. If we must converse with one another, let us speak about the honeysuckle, or my beautiful children, or your travels to Europe. Of the fashions, say, in Bucharest. Is it true that the Emperor Napoleon is in fact not much larger than a good-sized prairie dog?

ZACH: Why did you leave the masquerade?

EVA: For the same reason you went to Europe.

ZACH: To see Napoleon?

EVA: To spare my husband.

ZACH: He was not then your husband.

EVA: I was engaged.

ZACH: Then why did you let me embrace you?

EVA: Because I was engaged. All sixteen-year-old women are treacherous. All sixteen-year-old men are subhuman. The onset of sexual awareness is the end of human dignity. I am not, of course, actually speaking to you in this impossibly forward manner, you understand, so it's obvious to me that you must be hallucinating, and I will not stand here in the garden and be hallucinated upon. I am, after all, an excruciatingly respectable young woman.

ZACH: You're an extremely intelligent young woman.

EVA: I do hope the categories are not mutually exclusive. Do you make love to every intelligent woman you meet?

ZACH: I don't know. You're the first.

EVA: What a thoroughly revolting man you are. You're not going to kiss me, are you? Because I'm trembling so violently I fear that if you do, I shall be forced on principle to vomit on your shirt. Oh, God, I need to be somewhere else. Perhaps if I close my eyes and wish very hard I will awaken in Barbados.

ARMITAGE
Don Nigro

John Pendragon, thirty-five, sits in the library one autumn night in his father's Gothic mansion in east Ohio in 1845. Fay Morgan, sixteen, the housemaid, has just come into the library, unaware that John is there. John has been away to Yale and Europe but is back home, practicing law in a small town, lonely, unhappy, drinking a bit too much, and brooding about the death of his sister and his mother Eva's disappearance. Like his father Zach, John is very intelligent, with a sense of humor, but he also has a quality about him. Fay, the orphaned daughter of a barmaid, is smart, stubborn, respectful on the surface but determined not to be intimidated by these people. She is also, unknown to John, his father's illegitimate daughter. She loves the books and the house, and she wants them.

Fay has entered the library and is moving toward the bookshelves when John speaks from the shadows.

JOHN: Something I can do for you?

FAY: Jesus. You scared me to death. I'm sorry, sir. I didn't mean to blaspheme at you. I didn't know you were here. I'll come back at another time.

JOHN: Wait a minute. Don't run away.

FAY: I have work to do, sir.

JOHN: At night? What kind of work do you do at night? Why did you come in here?

FAY: I left something here.

JOHN: What?

FAY: I forgot. Excuse me, sir. I've really got to —

JOHN: You're not afraid of me, are you?

FAY: Certainly not.

JOHN: Then why have you been avoiding me ever since you came here?

FAY: Maybe I am just a bit afraid of you, sir.

JOHN: And why is that?

FAY: I don't know. Because you are older, perhaps.

JOHN: I'm thirty-five. That's not very old, is it? How old are you?

FAY: Sixteen.

JOHN: Ah. Then I am old, after all. I might have fathered you.

FAY: You've no right saying that. My mother was a good woman.

JOHN: I wasn't questioning your mother's virtue, I was lamenting my advanced age. You're not afraid of me because I'm thirty-five.

FAY: I'm afraid of you because I see violence in you.

JOHN: That's a rather odd thing for a servant girl to be telling the son of her master, don't you think?

FAY: You asked me, and I told you. May I go now?

JOHN: Do you think I'm going to do violence to you?

FAY: There are many kinds of violence.

JOHN: Where did you learn to talk like that?

FAY: What's wrong with the way I talk?

JOHN: You speak like an educated person.

FAY: I'm not stupid. I can read and write.

JOHN: Did your mother teach you that?

FAY: Yes.

JOHN: Do you like to read?

FAY: Yes. Very much.

JOHN: What did you read?

FAY: At home we had *Pilgrim's Progress, Robinson Crusoe, Gulliver's Travels,* Shakespeare, *Tom Jones, Tristram Shandy* —

JOHN: *Tristram Shandy* is not exactly a book for a proper young lady, is it?

FAY: Fortunately, sir, I am not a proper young lady. I'm just a poor servant girl. I think proper young ladies, if they can read at all, read the Bible, which is as full of violence and lechery as any book in the history of the world. I suppose that's what makes them so proper.

JOHN: You're rather a wicked girl aren't you?

FAY: Why? Because I can speak in complete sentences, without giggling and simpering like an idiot?

JOHN: I've noticed that a remarkably disproportionate amount of your time seems to be spent going in and out of this room.

FAY: The books get very dirty, sir.

JOHN: You like it in here, don't you?

FAY: I love all the rooms in this house, but I love this one the best, because the books live in here, and because it smells good and because of the way the sunlight falls there in the morning and there in the afternoon, and—

(She stops, looks at him, and sees she's said too much.)

JOHN: Do you read the books in this room when nobody's around?

FAY: Your father says I'm not to touch anything but dust.

JOHN: And God help us if we disobey my father.

FAY: Yes, sir. May I go now, sir?

JOHN: If you could read any one of these books, which would it be?

FAY: It's cruel of you to ask me such a question. You don't know how much pain it gives me, to see all these books here every day and not be allowed to read them.

JOHN: Answer the question.

FAY: I don't want to answer the question *(Pause.)* Byron.

JOHN: So you long to read Lord Byron, do you?

FAY: I will not be made fun of.

JOHN: Lord Byron was a wicked man.

FAY: So are you. I'm going now.

JOHN: Stop right there. *(She stops.)* You're not dismissed yet. You like to work at night. I've got some work for you.

FAY: What kind of work?

JOHN: Take down the red book there. That one. No, don't give it to me. Sit down. Right there. Sit down. I'm not going to bite you. *(She sits by the desk.)* Now, read to me.

FAY: You mean you never learned how to read, sir?

JOHN: I'm tired. I've been in town all day pretending to practice law, and my eyes hurt. Just read something.

FAY: From where?

JOHN: I don't care. Wherever you like. Come on.

FAY: You're not teasing me? *(She looks at him, hesitates, still suspicious, then opens the book as if it were a holy object, turns a page or two, and begins to read, very simply and very well:)*
So we'll go no more a-roving,
so late into the night,

though the heart be still loving,
and the moon be still as bright.
For the sword outwears its sheath,
and the soul wears out the breast,
and the heart must pause to breathe,
and love itself have rest.
Though the night was made for loving
and the day returns too soon,
yet we'll go no more a-roving
by the light of the moon.
(She looks up, sees him looking at her)

JOHN: You have a gift. That's good. You'll read to me every night, as part of your duties here. You decide what, I don't care, anything in this room right?

FAY: But your father —

JOHN: I'll take care of my father. So. Is it settled?

FAY: Whatever you like, sir?

JOHN: My name is John.

FAY: I know what your name is.

JOHN: Then call me by it.

FAY: All right.

JOHN: Good. Now, read me something else.

BEAST WITH TWO BACKS
Don Nigro

Al and Mary Margaret are both in their twenties. The play takes place in a Greenwich Village rooming house in 1927. Al is an aspiring artist who has recently rented a room. Mary Margaret is a "lost" actress from Ohio who live upstairs with her abusive boyfriend, Jem.

Their landlord, Mclish, has just exited.

MARY MARGARET: There is something wrong with him.

AL: There certainly is.

MARY MARGARET: No, I'm serious. He's sick or something. I know him.

AL: *(Retrieving the turkey from under the bed.)* He's all right.

MARY MARGARET: You shouldn't contradict a person who's just brought you a turkey.

AL: *(Sitting on the bed and taking the lid off.)* Are you sure you can spare this?

MARY MARGARET: Oh, yes. I'm temporarily wealthy. I got a job last week. I'll be rich for a least three more days.

AL: *(Sampling the turkey.)* Wow, this is great. An acting job?

MARY MARGARET: Advertisement. You'll soon be seeing my teeth in magazines all over the country. I was in a Prophylactic Toothbrush ad. Just teeth and my lips and a little gums and tongue to make it sexy. No chin, no nose. Once I got my whole face and arms and most of my torso in a saxophone ad. I had to hold this big old saxophone and look like I was blowing into it and smile at the same time, which is not easy. Girls! The stage door is open to you when you learn to play a Beuscher saxophone. Good pay on a year round vacation of travel and always a chance of stardom! — Saxophone aren't very comfortable. And one time I was a pirate in a silverware ad, and I wore this clingy tattered man's shirt and big old boots and not much else, except I had a blunderbuss, which is a gun with a funnel on the end you kill turkeys with, and I had a shovel and an earring and a scarf and I was wiping my forehead because I'd just dug up a chest of Johanna silverware, honest to God. Also I was Kelvinator Lady and a Grape Nuts Girl.

AL: That sounds like fun.

MARY MARGARET: It isn't, though. People treat you like a rump roast. They keep putting their hands all over me. I don't like people to be sticking their hands on me all the time unless they're people I want to. *(She looks at Al and then moves nervously away from him.)* So, do you want me to pose for you? I promised I would.

AL: You really want to?

MARY MARGARET: Sure, why not? Jem went to Coney Island. He needs to get away sometimes to write and be alone and, you know, suffer for his art and stuff.

AL: He went to Coney Island to suffer?

MARY MARGARET: I guess. Where do you want me to sit?

AL: Where would you feel comfortable?

MARY MARGARET: Oh, anyplace. I'm very flexible. Do you want me to take my clothes off?

AL: You don't have to take your clothes off.

MARY MARGARET: It's okay really.

AL: Well, you can if you want to.

MARY MARGARET: You don't want me to take my clothes off?

AL: No, that would be swell, but I don't want you to feel —

MARY MARGARET: You think I'm too skinny, don't you? Well, I can't help it. That's the style now. It's not my fault if you artists have a thing for fat women.

AL: I don't have a thing for fat women, I just —

MARY MARGARET: I mean, if you'd rather paint some woman who looks like Moby Dick or something, go right ahead. I didn't come down here to be insulted. I bring you all that white meat and stuffing and then you insult my body.

AL: I'm not insulting your body. You have a wonderful body. I love your body.

MARY MARGARET: That's okay, I've got to go, anyway. No hard feelings.

If I see any grotesquely bloated, cowlike women in the hallway I'll send them right in.

AL: Okay. Take off your clothes.

MARY MARGARET: You're just saying that to make be feel better.

AL: I don't want to make you feel better, I want you to take off your clothes.

MARY MARGARET: All of them?

AL: Yes. Every stitch. Come on, make it snappy.

MARY MARGARET: Boy, you artists are all alike. Everett warned me about people like you.

AL: So you don't want to take your clothes off?

MARY MARGARET: No. Why would I want to take my clothes off? What kind of girl do you think I am, anyway?

AL: At this point, I have no idea. What kind of a girl are you?

MARY MARGARET: A nice girl, who takes her clothes off when she feels like it. So do you want to paint me or what?

AL: First I draw, then I paint. Clothing is optional. Is that all right with you?

MARY MARGARET: Sure. Fine. So draw. *(She plunks herself down on the bed and assumes a rather affected pose.)* How's this?

AL: Relax.

MARY MARGARET: I am relaxing.

AL: Just be yourself.

MARY MARGARET: I don't want to be myself, I want to be a model.

AL: Look, don't pose, don't do anything, just sit there.

MARY MARGARET: Just sit here how?

AL: Are you sure you've done this before?

MARY MARGARET: Well, in advertisements they always want you to pretend something, and the last actual artist I posed for gave me two noses and a square head and told me to imagine I was the vortex of orgasm.

AL: Look, I'm not selling anything. I don't want a toothpaste lady or a pirate queen, or a girl with a square head. I just want YOU, all right?

MARY MARGARET: What for?

AL: So I can paint you.

MARY MARGARET: I thought you wanted to paint a picture.

AL: Yes, but of *you,* not some phony person you're trying to pretend you are.

MARY MARGARET: But I'm an actress. That's what acting is.

AL: No it's not.

MARY MARGARET: What are you, some sort of an expert or something? I'm a professional here, so don't try and tell me my business.

AL: Then don't try and tell me mine. Just relax, dammit, and act natural.

MARY MARGARET: Don't curse at me.

AL: Then sit still and shut up.

MARY MARGARET: Boy, what a grouch. You artists are really crabby. Okay, how about this?

(She strikes an even more affected pose.)

AL: I don't think this is going to work.

MARY MARGARET: Great. I didn't want to do it anyway.

AL: Yes you did, or you wouldn't have offered.

MARY MARGARET: I was just trying to be a good neighbor. I don't know what you're getting so mad about. I just want to be somebody interesting for you.

AL: Then be yourself.

MARY MARGARET: But I'm boring.

AL: You're not boring.

MARY MARGARET: You don't know me well enough yet. If you knew what I was really like, trust me, you'd be bored.

AL: You know you're not boring. You've just spent the last five minutes playing with me like a cat with a large mouse.

MARY MARGARET: I wasn't playing with you.

AL: You have no intention of taking your clothes off.

MARY MARGARET: How the hell do you know? Why don't you take *your* clothes off? How come it's only the model that's got to take her clothes off? I think the artist should have to work naked, too.

AL: All right. Fine.

(He starts unbuckling his belt.)

MARY MARGARET: No, never mind, forget it. STOP. All right. I'll try. I'll act normal, I swear.

AL: Okay.

(A moment. She tries.)

MARY MARGARET: Well, stop looking at me.

AL: How can I draw you if I don't look at you?

MARY MARGARET: The guy that gave me two noses didn't look at me.

AL: I'm not giving you two noses.

MARY MARGARET: This is hard. I can't.

AL: It's not hard.

MARY MARGARET: I think it's hard.

AL: *(Sighing and sitting down beside her.)* Look. Why don't you just try and, uh, describe yourself. Tell me who you are.

MARY MARGARET: I'm Mary Margaret Duncan, from East Liverpool, Ohio. It's on the river. We have rats.

AL: I know. I was there once.

MARY MARGARET: Oh, come on. Nobody goes to East Liverpool.

AL: Everybody on the bus from Cleveland to Pittsburgh does. Now, what else?

MARY MARGARET: What else what? Oh. Well, I'm twenty-five years old, but I look much younger. I look way too young to get good parts, it's terrible, they keep wanting to burp me, except for the sex maniacs, and they're *all* sex maniacs, they won't cast me but they sure want to screw me. Art is a rough business, and so is being a girl. But anyway, I weigh a hundred and something and a half pounds, almost, and, uh, how tall am I? Are you sure you were really in East Liverpool? You sure it wasn't Steubenville or Salineville or Salisbury or —

AL: Stop changing the subject.

MARY MARGARET: Well, I'm stuck.

AL: You're doing fine, just keep going.

MARY MARGARET: I read in the *Saturday Evening Post* that the people you love and the people who love you are the ones that tend to provide your self-definition. For example, Jem loves me, and he does define me — he says I'm stupid.

AL: I don't think you're stupid.

MARY MARGARET: Yes, but you don't love me, so that doesn't count. McLish loves me, sort of, like a dirty old grandfather, but I'm not sure what he actually thinks of me. Rachel loves me. She says I should sleep with a greater variety of people to broaden my outlook, but I don't know if that's a good idea or not. Everett loves me, but he doesn't talk about it. My parents used to love me, before I moved to New

York, but now they think I'm a shameless, fallen woman. You know, living in sin and all.

AL: Does that mean they stopped loving you?

MARY MARGARET: I don't know. They stopped sending money.

AL: Why did you come here?

MARY MARGARET: To be closer to Everett, so I could go see him. And because in East Liverpool you know pretty much what you're going to turn into. I didn't want to know. So I came here, and I was kind of lost for a while, and then Jem took me in.

AL: And?

MARY MARGARET: And that's who I am. Somebody Jem took in.

AL: You're a lot more than that. You sell yourself short, you do it all the time, and you do it on purpose. Why do you do that?

MARY MARGARET: I think maybe you just take me too seriously. You shouldn't take people so seriously. That'll get you into lots of trouble, and most people aren't worth it, although it's kind of nice that you should bother to care one way or the other, even though technically it's none of your business, of course. So, who are you?

AL: I'm the guy who's going to paint your picture.

MARY MARGARET: Ah. So you define yourself through your work. Now, is that really you, or is it just a role you play because secretly you're really boring, like me?

AL: Maybe I hide behind it sometimes, but it's still who I am.

MARY MARGARET: Why?

AL: Uh. Well, it's a way of, I don't know, capturing things. Moments. Everything in time is mortal, goes away, dies, disappears, eludes one. Painting is a way of keeping things.

MARY MARGARET: No. Keeping is a lie.

(She looks at her hands. He looks at her.)

AL: Now you're natural. I can draw that.

(He starts up.)

MARY MARGARET: *(Pulling him back by the arm.)* Don't go over there.

AL: All right.

(A moment. He moves to kiss her.)

MARY MARGARET: No, I don't want you doing that, either. I just want you right here close for a minute, okay?

AL: Okay.

MARY MARGARET: Don't you wonder sometimes if what you do is really — I mean, what's the point? What good does it do anybody? Do you know what I mean? Sometimes I wonder that about what I do. It seems kind of selfish.

AL: *(Reaching for a book.)* Here. Look at this. This is my favorite artist. He's Norwegian. His name is Edvard Munch.

MARY MARGARET: *(Turning over the pages.)* Wow. These are very weird. Oh, I love this one. What does it mean?

AL: I don't know. What do you see?

MARY MARGARET: Well, there's this girl, she's very pretty, and she's wearing a white dress, and there's all these couples dancing, but she hasn't danced yet, she's shy, I guess, but she wants to, so eventually she does, because here she is, dancing with this guy, only now she's wearing a red dress, she's part of the dance now, only she doesn't look happy, there's something creepy about this guy, like the one in the background with this other girl, it's like he wants to suck her blood or something, and then here she is again, only now she's in a black dress, and her hands are folded, and she's watching the dance, like looking at herself in the past, but she won't dance again, ever. This is a wonderful picture.

AL: *(Showing her another book.)* Look at this. Peter Brueghel. And this. John Everett Millais, *Autumn Leaves.* Turner. Look at the light. John Singer Sargent. Look, this is Renoir. He had arthritis so bad, he had them tie the brush to his hand in the morning so he could paint. Now, what was the point of that? What makes a thing not worth doing is if you're half not doing it, so there are dead spaces in your soul where you know you should care but you don't. If you can do what gives joy without half not doing it and without hurting anybody, whose right is it to pass judgment? Life is short, do what you love, and don't let anybody stop you, that's what I think.
(She looks at him. Then she kisses him. She kisses him again. More involvement. She leans herself back, allows, encourages, and it begins to grow serious. Then, rather suddenly, she is crying.)

MARY MARGARET: I think you better just leave me alone.

AL: What's wrong?

MARY MARGARET: Just get your filthy hands off me.

> *(He pulls away.)*

AL: I'm sorry. I thought —

MARY MARGARET: *(Sitting up, wiping her eyes with her hands and straightening her clothes.)* I don't know why we always end up in bed. We were in bed together even before we met. Why does that keep happening?

AL: I know why it happens. I haven't figured out yet why it stops.

MARY MARGARET: *(Getting up.)* I have to go now. Don't keep your turkey under the bed or the mice will drag it into the closet. Good-bye. *(She goes out the door.)*

BOYS AND GIRLS
Tom Donaghy

This is an incisive comedy about same-sex parenting. Bev and Reed (thirties) were once lovers; but now he has a boyfriend (well, he's on the outs with him) and Bev is one-half of a same-sex couple. Bev and her girlfriend have a baby. Now, they feel they need someone to play the role of the baby's father. Bev wants Reed to oblige.

BEV: God, we were children. We were drinking way too much, I put on all that weight.

REED: You look great.

BEV: I'm down twenty.

REED: So am I.

BEV: Lean and mean.

REED: We were kids.

BEV: She's not jealous.

REED: There's something —

BEV: No —

REED: Not on my end. On hers.

BEV: It's history, no —

REED: A feeling.

BEV: It's natural. And it's over. That's when we met and she was wondering — you and I spent all that time together and everyone had to adjust, struggle. There's a little brutality there when loves comes into the picture. She's very fond of you, that's the point. Very. She loves who I love. Now she's secure enough to love who I love. There was a little bloodletting there, but that's — of all our friends — the friends we have everywhere — you stand in a class, a different class. A class apart. We, you know, cherish you. The struggle's over and we're all a little punch-drunk, but still standing.

REED: It upsets her that you and I screwed.

BEV: Just twice. Well, what can you do? Do you want to see the sconce now?

REED: I really haven't been drinking that much anymore.

BEV: She knows that.

REED: Those stories get around.

BEV: She knows

REED: With all the work it's impossible —

BEV: She's just against anything she perceives as a fault. A character fault, a flaw. She's clean and good and she makes me sturdy. I'm not some kid wandering around at dusk with a six-pack anymore. Peeing on sofas. Sleeping with boys. I haven't peed on anyone's sofa in ten years!

REED: Sure I'll see the sconce.

(He moves to go; Bev doesn't follow.)

REED: *(Continued.)* What?

BEV: We want you to live with us.

(A moment passes in silence.)

REED: What?

BEV: He needs a father.

REED: Who?

(Another silence.)

REED: *(Continued.)* Is he asleep?

BEV: He's asleep now, yeah. He usually goes down around nine. We're trying to make it earlier and tonight he fell for it. He's got this little doll, this monkey if you dangle it long enough it has a hypnotic effect. *(Beat.)* He's four — he knows everything. He knows the whole setup, so it's not an illusion, to *create* one — a father or a male — he's asking about men. What they're like when they're around. Not for sports or jockey things — but how they're different. He's got all these women and he's great and they love him but there's something else. He knows it.

REED: We've been through this way back.

BEV: No, that was different, that was sperm!

REED: Yes, and it's not mine!

BEV: Shell thinks we have to do something. And I'm in agreement. All around. You look in his eyes and you want to answer that. *(Looks into her wineglass.)* I'm having more, how are you?

REED: Fine.

BEV: You don't want that beer?

REED: No.

BEV: *(She pours herself more wine.)* You want to, um, satisfy whatever you see. In his eyes, whatever that is. Where's Daddy is too complicated to get into. Who ever knows really? But men — that's an easier question to answer. They're everywhere! We just need one to come over the house every now and then.

REED: And what am I doing?

BEV: During daylight hours.

REED: I come over in the day! And the rest — the official — the title or formal title — there's no room for that. *(Beat.)* I don't know how to say this without —

BEV: Say it.

REED: — something meager —

BEV: No —

REED: — mean or —

BEV: *(Simultaneous with Reed's next line.)* — no — no — no — no — no — say it.

REED: — and I know we're supposed to be creating — I know all that, what you're trying to do here, everything you're building, and you two are great and totally sufficient I'm sure —

BEV: Say it!

REED: I am! I'm saying the whole thing sounds like a minefield.

BEV: Break it down.

REED: It's a minefield!

BEV: We need sturdiness, that's all I'm saying. And you're single now after Jason and we have these empty rooms — rent-free by the by — and he's asking me where the men are. Rent-free and "Where are the men, Mommy?" and *rent-free*.

REED: Everything doesn't have to be a list.

BEV: It's not a list.

REED: Checking off things —

BEV: It's not a fucking list —

REED: — sconce, faucet, daddy! *(Beat.)* No, but I'm sorry.

BEV: I got it.

REED: No, I am, I'm sorry — some people don't get everything.

BEV: Okay, drop it.

REED: *(Beat.)* I just don't want it to come up again. Like I'm somehow lacking. Like I'm some freak because I don't want children.

BEV: I thought you did — ?

REED: People who want children are the only people who should have them.

BEV: But you always said — ?

REED: I hated it, being young. I hated it. So what am I supposed to convey to a kid? And what about when do I get to be carefree? My mother — being the oldest, all that — when am I allowed to be — have my carefree time? I'm not gonna turn around just when I have some semblance of —

BEV: Fine.

REED: — freedom —

BEV: Fine.

REED: I'm not, I'm sorry — I am. It would work out well. It would.

BEV: It would.

REED: I know. But I don't want it. He's lovely, he's great. I have a crush, with his pictures, and I quote all his little things to people, his little things he says about poop and monsters, go around like some suburban mom saying Georgie said blah blah —

BEV: He's verbal.

REED: He's very verbal.

BEV: He is.

REED: I know, he talks. I'm saying he is. And I like that in a kid. I know what he's thinking. The ones who don't talk, they spook the fuck out of me! Staring there with their eyes, judging me or something, feeling superior, knowing I don't know shit, little devil children. Hester Prynne's kid. The power they have. The power they have over you. *(Beat.)* Which can be . . . fun. Sometimes. A kid can be a lot of . . . It's just I — I wanted one with Jason.

BEV: Okay.

CARL THE SECOND
Marc Palmieri

Carl Fraser (twenties to thirties) manages a used bookstore and identifies with the also-rans of literature whose books he sells. Enter Christine (twenties to thirties), perhaps the first woman he's ever met who doesn't think he's a nobody.

Carl and Christine stand in pools of light.

CHRISTINE: Hello?

CARL: Hello? Christine?

CHRISTINE: Yes.

CARL: It's Carl.

CHRISTINE: Carl!

CARL: So. I got your message and, so, that was what? Two? No. Yes. It was too . . . it was today.

CHRISTINE: Yes!

CARL: So I'm . . . I guess . . . you know? I can't speak. Forget it. Bye.

CHRISTINE: Carl?

CARL: Yes.

CHRISTINE: *Est-ce que vous voudriez boire quelque chose avec moi?*

CARL: What?

CHRISTINE: Would you like to have a drink with me?

CARL: Ah! Yes. *Bon!* When? Tonight?

CHRISTINE: Sure. Where?

CARL: Well, there's a place on Sixth Street that I like. Actually I'm standing here right now, but I could leave, then come back.

CHRISTINE: Okay. Or just wait there.

CARL: Okay.

CHRISTINE: What's the place?

CARL: Sixth Street?

CHRISTINE: Right. What's the name of the place?

CARL: Oh. Yes. That would be good. Café Lulu. Sixth between First and Second.

CHRISTINE: Great. What time?

CARL: Whenever. I mean, I'm here now so, whenever.

CHRISTINE: I can be there by seven. Good?

CARL: That's . . . that's . . .*(Carl and Christine move to two chairs and sit, as if at a café. He holds out an old newspaper clipping.)* That's me. Right back there.

CHRISTINE: No!

CARL: Yes. And behind me there, in the background, is a gigantic portrait of my brother Ron. His chin was bigger than the scoreboard. He was a legend in that gym. But this was my finest hour. The great assist.

CHRISTINE: Wow. That's very moving. Thank you for that.

CARL: Sure. Now, how did you get into coaching basketball?

CHRISTINE: Well I was interviewing for teacher positions and, well, at this school they asked me if I could coach any sports so, hell, I said hoops.

CARL: Right, because you're . . . ?

CHRISTINE: I'm the youngest of three. Two older brothers who played in high school. When I was little if they needed an extra person to even out the two-on-twos in the driveway, there I was. So I'm qualified enough.

CARL: Are you close to your family?

CHRISTINE: I don't know. I guess so. My brothers are dear to me. I've made a sort of lifestyle out of rooting for them. Now it's softball. They're all about their big softball dynasty. It's a sweet part of our life, I guess. I go and watch them play. I'm the team groupie, I guess. They're really good.

CARL: That's great.

CHRISTINE: Are you close to your family?

CARL: Ah, well, you've heard the old saying, "There's nothing better than family . . . in another country." They're in this country, but the shoe fits.

CHRISTINE: *(Laughing.)* Okay.

CARL: Well we should have a little one-on-one. One-on-one there's nobody to pass the ball to so I'd be forced to shoot. That'd be redeeming, maybe.

CHRISTINE: You're on.

CARL: Good. *(A beat.)*

CHRISTINE: So I'm glad you called me.

CARL: Me too.

CHRISTINE: I kinda asked you out, though.

CARL: You did, didn't you.

CHRISTINE: 'Cause you couldn't talk.

CARL: Yeah. Sorry about that. I meant to. I would have.

CHRISTINE: I liked it.

CARL: You did?

CHRISTINE: Yeah. I did. I think I'll do it again. *(A beat.)*

CARL: To me or just again?

CHRISTINE: Wanna see me again?

CARL: Yes! And there is the one-on-one game.

CHRISTINE: Oh yeah.

CARL: See with the game idea I kind of asked you out. It was oblique and sneaky but I did do it. I think.

CHRISTINE: So now we're' going out twice more.

CARL: We are booked well in advance right now.

CHRISTINE: Then you know what that makes this?

CARL: What?

CHRISTINE: The first date.

CARL: Ooh. I guess so, Well, how does it rank up? In your career of first date? One through ten.

CHRISTINE: Ten's the highest?

CARL: Yeah.

CHRISTINE: Ten.

CARL: Really!

CHRISTINE: Sure. Why not. What about you? How does this rank in your career?

CARL: Oh, no, I only remember last dates. Anyway, my career's been kind of idle for a while.

CHRISTINE: Oh yeah? Why? Some big drama?

CARL: No, no. Big? No. My romantic life could best be described as a collection of bad short stories. Real short. Haikus. What about you. How's your library?

CHRISTINE: Oh, some short stories. One in novel form.

CARL: Yeah? How many pages?

CHRISTINE: About three years worth. I was engaged once. Six months from having a husband. There wasn't a soul who knew him that didn't tell me, "He's the one! You're so lucky! You two are perfect for each other!"

CARL: What happened?

CHRISTINE: I realized one day, just looking at him, that for the first time I actually looked at him for myself. Alone. No cheerleaders. No counselors. Just me. I didn't see anything I wanted in him. Nothing. And it was over. And everyone was so shocked. Everyone but us.

CARL: He felt the same?

CHRISTINE: Exactly. Thank God. It was the biggest relief. For me.

CARL: And me. *(Carl rises and turns to the audience, lights shift as he does to illuminate the bookstore area, where Christine begins to wander, as if studying the shelves. To audience.)* A week goes by. I sit in the bleachers and watch her run practice. The players giggle and point at me. We find a rusty old hoop in the Village and play our one-on-one. I lose on a questionable foul call. She comes to the store for my Dickens Society meeting, where I read passages of *The Old Curiosity Shop* to three ladies in their nineties who, because they are sleeping, don't notice I've placed the book down as Nell is wandering through the graveyard, to make out with Christine in the philosophy section. I ride the subway and stare everywhere in rapture, and even in the blackened dirty windows I see her face. And my breath goes short and my stomach is light.

CHRISTINE: You know what?

(Carl, now in the bookstore area but still lingering in the pleasure of his last speech, watches her in admiration.)

CHRISTINE: Carl.

CARL: Yeah.

CHRISTINE: This must be a nice place to work every day. At my job I'm surrounded by people. Kids, other teachers, parents. It never ends. I'm in the middle of so many lives at once. I'm never alone. This is

different. Quiet. Still. You're lucky. *(She pulls a book.)* To A God Unknown.

CARL: Early Steinbeck.

CHRISTINE: What's it about?

CARL: Oh, man's degrading struggle in the universe of a silent God.

CHRISTINE: Do you believe that God is silent?

CARL: Oh, no. I constantly hear him booing me. *(She replaces the book.)*

CHRISTINE: You know, I consider myself a fairly well-read person but there's
nothing to humble you like a bookstore. It's endless. You can't possibly read everything.

CARL: Who'd want to?

CHRISTINE: You would.

CARL: No. Yuck. I hate books.

CHRISTINE: See, now why do you say that?

CARL: Say what?

CHRISTINE: Why do you mock something you love? You've probably read
everything in this fiction section, and you say you hate books. What's
your problem? You mock your job. You mock your degree. You mock
your passion.

CARL: Do I do that?

CHRISTINE: Yes. And I don't like it.

CARL: I don't know.

CHRISTINE: You love it so much it scares you. Is that it? One of those deals?

CARL: No.

CHRISTINE: Well, there will be no more mocking! Okay?

CARL: Okay. *(She kisses him, then turns back toward the shelves.)*

CHRISTINE: *Moby Dick.* That's a whopper. We were assigned it in high
school. I skippethed it. What's it about?

CARL: Oh, God.

CHRISTINE: Tell me.

CARL: Well, a big whale.

CHRISTINE: Thanks. I want your summary. Why is it a classic? What's the
big deal? What's the guy's name again? The captain?

CARL: Ahab.

CHRISTINE: Ahab. With the peg leg.

CARL: Right. And *Moby Dick* is . . . *Moby Dick* is a lot of things.

CELLINI
John Patrick Stanley

The Italian Renaissance sculptor Benvenuto Cellini (forties) is sketching a model named Caterina (twenties), who is also his mistress, and who wants more money.

Caterina, beautiful, appears washing with a bowl and pitcher. Cellini immediately switches to sketching her. She carelessly uncovers her naked-ness, splashes herself, and recovers.

CATERINA: Do you never tire of drawing me?

CELLINI: Never! In Paris, I had a model named Caterina.

CATERINA: You had her, and had her.

CELLINI: I would take her as my image for the Medusa.

[BOY: Was she beautiful?]

CELLINI: What's a model if not for beauty?

CATERINA: I am very beautiful. I am exceptionally beautiful.

CELLINI: I am in love with her.

CATERINA: Why?

CELLINI: I see God's finest work in you. I see the stars in you, the black earth that feeds us, the soft milk of giving love. I will see your face as in a magic crystal on the day of my death, and remember your skin, your hair, the sound of your voice.

CATERINA: But then, Benvenuto, don't you think you should give me more money?

CELLINI: Money.

CATERINA: Just a little more.

CELLINI: How can you do this?

CATERINA: My mother needs to pay her rent.

CELLINI: I speak of the profoundest feelings I have yet known and you speak of money.

CATERINA: I must be practical. If not for myself, then at least for my family.

CELLINI: There is nothing practical about being a prostitute.

CATERINA: Call it what you like. I need more money.

CELLINI: I call it what it is! I call it what every man and woman in Paris calls it! I call it prostitution!

CATERINA: Fine! Then pay up and I'll bend over! Is that pretty enough?

CELLINI: Pretty is as pretty does! You are not pretty! You have the sensibility of a Gorgon and your mother is a red-chafed elbow of the Devil!

CATERINA: We have to protect ourselves!

CELLINI: From what?!

CATERINA: The day of your indifference!

CELLINI: You invite that day!

CATERINA: Say what you want. You love me. I can feel the pull.

CELLINI: Love. What a word for something so wasteful and base. I take your body for my subject and my appetite. If I could hack away your disgusting nature, it would be out with the scraps!

CATERINA: My nature is my attraction.

CELLINI: Your nature divides me against myself!

CATERINA: *You* are divided against yourself and blame whoever's handy!

CELLINI: Very well! Then I'm alone and you are a madness of mine!

CATERINA: I am no man's madness however mad the man! This is why my mother never trusted you!

CELLINI: Your mother.

CATERINA: We knew you would use me and never know me.

CELLINI: I know you.

CATERINA: No. I know *you!* You are ignorant of the Female! And as arrogant as you are unenlightened! Look at the women in your work! They are unfuckable!

CELLINI: You describe yourself.

CATERINA: Then why do you fuck me?!

CELLINI: I try to love you. What is this blindness that makes me speak the language of innocence to a whore? When will I be cured, and how?

CATERINA: You are not a man.

CELLINI: Don't take that route! Remember! My work will save you from death!

CATERINA: The part you'll save I can do without.

CELLINI: Can we stop?!

CATERINA: *Arrête quoi?*

CELLINI: Fighting!

CATERINA: It's only because you're cheap.

CELLINI: Be tender with me! Please!

CATERINA: I don't feel like it. You make me sick.

CELLINI: If only you could embrace the good between us!

CATERINA: I do. But the good between us is *bad.*

CELLINI: You're blind.

CATERINA: That may be! But if I'm sightless then you are senseless altogether! Not to know the truth of us! You insist I make a fool of you and so I will! I would've been content to have you paw me and pay me! But you won't rest until I humiliate you for calling this arrangement Love!

CELLINI: Stop it!

CATERINA: And as for your Art, no man glued to the nipple will ever be great!

CELLINI: Leave off!

CATERINA: You will leave no mark!

CELLINI: Don't say it! *(He slaps her. She sobs.)* Don't say that. *(She runs away crying.)* Run away and cry like a little girl! You know you'll come back!

CATERINA: Never, you pig, never! *(She's gone. He calls after.)*

CELLINI: Nothing will be wasted! Not even this. My Medusa.

DIRTY BLONDE
Claudia Shear

Jo and Charlie (both thirties) have an important thing in common: They
both are obsessed by Mae West. Charlie works in the archives of the New
York Public Library.

JO: I grew up in a world of women — my father left when I was little,
    my mother never remarried, I only had sisters, I went to a Catholic
    girls school — men were like foreign creatures to me — they fright-
    ened me. They frighten me now. That's why it's so nice with Char-
    lie. I know he likes me, looks forward to my arrival, looks up as the
    elevator dings, as the door opens, just to see if it's me. One time I
    went by the archives and as I came in I saw him looking at his re-
    flection in a window, and he was . . . fixing his shirt. And I thought
    "Oh, that's for me, he's fixing it for me." Like being given a present.
    (Charlie, having entered during Jo's speech, looks out.)
CHARLIE: It started out with an intense affection for Halloween. I always
    went as a vampire. I loved the makeup on my face, I loved my mouth
    all red. I would do that last of all, standing in the bathroom, shiv-
    ering with excitement as my mother leaned over me with her golden
    tube of lipstick, me looking at her, her looking at me, her mouth
    pouting a little, mirroring mine. I would turn and look into the mir-
    ror over the sink — not smile, just look and swoosh my cape back
    and forth, back and forth and then let go and the momentum kept
    it flying and . . . "whhht" wrapped around me. Haaaa.
    (Lights change.)

ARCHIVES, MID-OCTOBER

JO: You know the guy that's always in the reading room, he wears sweat-
    pants and *yarn* around his ponytail?
CHARLIE: Oh, the Pasolini freak.

JO: He shussed me! I was reading "The Drag" and I laughed for a second and he shussed me!

CHARLIE: What did you do?

JO: Blew him a kiss. He turned around really quickly.

(Jo and Charlie sit together. Charlie takes out two miniature Almond Joy candy bars.)

CHARLIE: Want one?

JO: I thought you couldn't have food here! You freaked on me about the iced coffee.

(Charlie breathes a small patient sigh.)

CHARLIE: I didn't *freak,* you're so dramatic. *(Hands her one.)* Somebody brought them in for Halloween.

(Jo unwraps it.)

JO: I *love* Halloween. I love candy, I love dressing up — I once saw a girl on the L train with a tinfoiled box around her head and two wires sticking up with pieces of bread attached. She was going as a toaster. *(Jo takes a bite of the candy.)* YUM — the aptly named Almond Joy.

CHARLIE: "Almond, joy of man's desiring."

JO: God, I miss trick or treating. I remember my sister and I dumping our entire shopping bag of candy on the playroom floor and just *pawing* through it.

CHARLIE: What did you go as?

JO: My sister was once a flower girl and she got to wear a white tulle dress with a hoop skirt. I wore that every Halloween. Even when it was really ratty and tight. What did you go as?

CHARLIE: *(Abruptly.)* Vampire. *(Changing the subject.)* There's a party here next week for Halloween.

JO: Like an office party?

CHARLIE: No, a party party — a big charity thing. Wanna go?

JO: Thanks, I'd love to — is it dressy?

CHARLIE: Dress *up* — it's a costume party.

JO: Yeah? Oh, I haven't been to a costume party since college —

CHARLIE: You could go as . . .

CHARLIE and JO: Mae.

(Jo giggles nervously.)

JO: You think?

CHARLIE: Sure.

JO: No, I mean, you think?

    (She's dying to be persuaded.)

CHARLIE: *Yeah.*

JO: I could get a cheap wig on 14th Street.

CHARLIE: I've got some stuff.

JO: I'm so psyched. What are you gonna go as?

CHARLIE: A guy in a tie.

JO: You can't just go as a guy in a tie.

CHARLIE: Okay, a guy in a tie with a mask.

JO: Why won't you dress up?

CHARLIE: *(Uncharacteristically abrupt.)* Because I won't. D'you still want to go?

JO: Okay. Okay. Sure.

CHARLIE: You're gonna be a great Mae! Do you want to come over on Saturday? We'll get everything together, drink a little wine. Do a trial run.

JO: Okay, I'll see you then.

    (Charlie exits. Jo looks out.)

JO: So, Saturday rolled around, I got to Charlie's apartment, I started to get ready and I had to go to the bathroom. Well, I came out and I saw a box in his bedroom I thought was my stuff. I reached in and pulled out a white satin skirt and held it up and without thinking I ran into the living room . . .

    (Jo exits.)

CHARLIE'S APARTMENT

Charlie carries on a dressing screen and a shopping bag.

JO: *(Offstage.)* Charlie! This is so *big!* I am bumming out! Is *this* how fat you think I am! I mean, when you look at me, is this how big I look to you?

    (Jo enters holding up a large skirt. Charlie is standing in front of her. He freezes, doesn't answer. She freezes. They stare at each other for a

moment. *Without speaking he takes the skirt from her. He hands her the bag.)*

CHARLIE: *(Quietly.) This* is your stuff.

JO: Oh. Oh. Oh. *(Jo turns out.) Ohhh.* Well, I mean. I didn't care. So, he's not just gay *as* a handbag, he's gay *with* a handbag.
(Lights shift to Charlie.)

CHARLIE: *(To the audience.)* What was I thinking? You leave the *dress* in the *box,* the box in the *closet* and you keep the door *shut. (Stops, considers.)* But she didn't run out screaming. And I'm not dead.
(Charlie exits.)

JO: I put on a CD, started opening a bottle of wine. Charlie came back into the room and it was okay, the moment passed.

ENDPAPERS
Thomas McCormack

Joshua Maynard, the old and regal owner of Joshua Maynard Books, has abruptly died, leaving the house in the hands of his twenty-seven-year-old daughter, Sara. She knows her first job is to find someone to run the publishing house. In this scene she is interviewing Griff, thirty-eight to forty-two, a smart, gifted editor. Griff feels he must accept the assignment if Sara asks him to, but, for personal reasons, he hopes it doesn't come to that. So, with all due courtesy, he is trying to convey he is not the right man.

Lights up on Josh's office. Sara and Griff.

SARA: I don't want to be the publisher.

GRIFF: Why not?

SARA: I just spent two weeks in my father's study reading forty years of his speeches and letters — and private handwritten memos to himself. Learned . . . many things . . . When Dad was in his big easy-chair reading, it seemed like a gorgeous way of life. Books! My best pals! But a year here showed there's a lot more to it than just reading books.

GRIFF: When was that?

SARA: The year I was twenty-three . . . I'm twenty-seven.

GRIFF: You were right out of college?

SARA: *(Shakes head.)* After college I went to England, to acting school. I broke new ground in awful. After England, I worked here, and after that, law school for a year. Then I went on the road, and on the Riviera, and finally on the roofs of Mississippi. Lots of travel, exposure to all kinds of work. I was proud of the Mississippi time, but none of it came close to saying, "*This* is where you belong." . . . So for this house I need a foster parent. Someone knowledgeable, numeric, literate . . . and decent.

GRIFF: You've got a board of directors. Let them find someone.

SARA: No. Dad used to hold one board meeting a year, at our home, over dinner. Then brandy and cigars — masking the smell of the rubber stamp. They were just his cronies, from Harvard and his clubs. I doubt they could name a single employee except Ida and Ralph. This one decision I have to make. Did you enjoy teaching?

GRIFF: . . . I taught at a citadel of literacy. Here's how literate. One day I saw a *grad* student arrive at school to find his luggage had been crushed. He opened the bag, and this articulate Ivy League scholar announced, "My shit got fucked!" In the beginning I enjoyed it. Then came a time . . . when I wanted a change of scene.

SARA: Were you one of those competitive academics? Publishing more papers than the next guy? *(Griff studies Sara with seeming wariness.)* I'm just asking a colleague questions. Help me — you're ready to help everyone else.

GRIFF: *(Ponders; then mock fatuous pride.)* . . . I wrote published papers of heroic unintelligibility.

SARA: Like what?

GRIFF: *(Continues comic tone.)* Like one advancing a radical ideational theory of meaning.

SARA: Oh I'm mad about theories of meaning!

GRIFF: I said meanings have no ontic status in a text, only in minds, as stimulated notions which are indeterminate, non-unitary, non-discrete, and transitory. That's what I said.

SARA: *(Mock chiding.)* Oh you didn't!

GRIFF: *(High comic smugness.)* Yes I did . . . *(Back to serious.)* I wrote papers, but I didn't show them around. I had an undeserved reputation as the department nice-guy — I seemed so understanding and non-competitive. And I *was* non-competitive, because I *did* understand — and what I understood was that none of my colleagues was worth arguing with. Which was good because there was a part of me poised to attack like a rabid wolf. Trouble is, you're liable to get a reputation as a good listener if you see little point in talking yourself.

SARA: Has editing been better?

GRIFF: What part? When I read the slush, it's like working at a clinic for the incurable. When I edit? Last month I sent an author his script —

with two-thousand-two-hundred suggested, *necessary, obvious* corrections. On a self-pitying day, I feel shackled — a galley slave, because if I know I can fix it, I know I must fix it.

SARA: You're shackled to helping people — a virtue, no?

GRIFF: Up to a point.

SARA: . . . Did you envy my father?

GRIFF: No. David Hume said, envy requires proximity — if the object is too removed from you, the question of comparison does not arise. The philosopher, he said, does not envy the tycoon.

SARA: It's a powerful job. Some people want power.

GRIFF: Some. Others might crave the money, or the prestige.

SARA: There's no one who might simply want to prevent harm and do good? . . . Could you do that — prevent harm and do good?

GRIFF: Have you talked to Ted?

SARA: Could you work for him?

GRIFF: I could certainly *start* to work for him.

SARA: You like him? Admire him?

GRIFF: Ted has a definable excellence: Based on information and savvy, he makes things happen. Absent *that* talent, all other talents are wasted. Granted, the doctor's rule also applies to editors and CEOs. First *do* no harm.

SARA: You should have been a doctor.

GRIFF: Ah, no. And if I were, I'd choose research, avoid patients.

SARA: But you're so good with — the needy.

GRIFF: Ever think of the sense of duty as an immune deficiency?

SARA: . . . Sometimes you sound like two different people.

GRIFF: Because I *am* two. I'm malformed. A twinful egg did not divide. The warm, helpful doctor-teacher-editor is Siamesed to a cool, disdainful and pernicious brother. I'm involuntarily but constantly judgmental. The way others see colors, I see insufficiencies — in others, in myself. So I'm angry when the needy depend on me, that I can't shrug them off, that eventually they'll want more than I can give, that I'll want more than *they* can give. I'm a ludicrous braid of Father Damien and Schopenhauer.

SARA: . . . The bankers tell me the company is in some peril. It's undercapitalized, they say, figuring I'm not sure what it means — make me anxious and I'll be easier to steer, I'll choose a businessman, not a Catcher in the Rye.

GRIFF: Old Holden looked doomed to a life of discontent.

SARA: . . . These last happy, terrible five months with Dad, he was like his Havana smoke, passing into his own bindings. *(Gazes at fourth wall of books.)* See? Joshua Maynard . . . Books. Thank you, Griff. *(Exit Griff.)*

FORTUNE'S FOOL
Ivan Turgenev, adapted by Mike Poulton

Kuzovkin, an impoverished aristocrat, has been living on the charity of Olga's father, who has recently died, at his country estate. Olga has come to claim the inheritance. Here, Kuzovkin tells about how he came to be a ward of her father's, and he tells her the truth about who he really is (in relation to her). Kuzovkin is a middle-aged man (played by Alan Bates in the Broadway production). Olga is in her twenties.

Kuzovkin enters, pale and drawn. He reacts to the fact that she is sitting in the window and covers his reaction with difficulty.

OLGA: Good morning, Vassily Petrovitch.
(Kuzovkin bows.)

KUZOVKIN: Everything is arranged. Ivanov is here to collect me — I shall stay with him for a few days and then I'm ready to leave.

OLGA: Sit down, Vassily Petrovitch.

KUZOVKIN: Ask me to die for you.

OLGA: No, I won't ask that. Only tell me the truth. The truth forgives all. *(She pauses.)* I heard what you said.

KUZOVKIN: *(Poleaxed.)* What did you hear?

OLGA: *(Forcing herself.)* About me. Is it true?

KUZOVKIN: Oh.

OLGA: What is the truth?

KUZOVKIN: Let me go.

OLGA: *(Holding him.)* It won't do. No. For the love of God — the truth! Don't torture me. The truth! Tell me quickly.

KUZOVKIN: You ask . . .

OLGA: Is it true!

KUZOVKIN: *(Almost inaudible.)* Oh, let it come then. Yes, it's true. *(He sinks to his knees.)*
(Olga moves away quickly.)

OLGA: Get up. Please. *(She tries to appear hard.)*

KUZOVKIN: *(Getting off his knee.)* Olga Petrovna . . . .

OLGA: Sit here — on the sofa. *(Pause.)* Vassily Petrovitch . . . do you understand what you have said?

KUZOVKIN: I've spoken madness. Nothing but madness. I'll tell you what's true — I truly believe that I'm going out of my mind. Send me away before I do any more harm. I believe I no longer know what I'm saying.

OLGA: You know very well what you're saying. There's no going back now. You must tell me everything . . .

KUZOVKIN: How could I begin?

OLGA: Either you have slandered my mother — in which case you will leave this room this instant and never come near me again . . .

(He can't bring himself to go.)

OLGA: *You see, you can't do it. You can't do it!*

KUZOVKIN: Merciful God, merciful God . . . !

OLGA: I am in torment! Do you want that?

KUZOVKIN: Not for the world.

OLGA: *(Trying to smile.)* We must help each other.

KUZOVKIN: Yes. Yes. I see me must. *(He pauses.)* Only please don't look at me like that . . . I can't bear it . . . .

OLGA: *(Soothing.)* Vassily Petrovitch . . . I . . .

KUZOVKIN: *(Gently.)* My dear, forgive me, that's not my name. My name is Vassily Semyonitch . . .

(Embarrassed, Olga shrugs nervously, starting to tremble.)

OLGA: Oh. Vassily Semyonitch . . . You must think me . . . but you can't expect . . .

KUZOVKIN: *(Through tears.)* Don't be angry with me. I can't speak if you won't help me.

(Olga seems afraid of physical contact with him but she takes his hand; she is trying to keep control of her body.)

OLGA: You mustn't be afraid of me. I'm as frightened as you are. More so. Much, much more. Look at me. I'm shaking. One of us has to be calm.

KUZOVKIN: It won't be me.

OLGA: I'll be still — very still — and you will begin at the beginning. Like the stories you used . . .

KUZOVKIN: Oh! *(After a tremendous effort.)* I was just twenty. No money. Rotten education. Your father . . .

(Olga shudders.)

KUZOVKIN: The man you call your father — may God be merciful to him — came to my rescue or I should have been destitute — brought me here, to this house, said he'd find a government post for me . . . It didn't happen . . . I just sort of stayed on. I'd been living here for — oh, about two years — when he met and married your mother. She was — I believe this with my soul, with my whole being — an angel. Before you were born . . . *(He pauses.)* Before you were born there were two little boys . . . neither of them lived very long, poor things — how she loved them! And after their deaths . . . How can I say it? Her husband was a vicious man. There are no words that would make that truth any easier to tell. Vicious and terrible; there were times, rages, when he seemed possessed by devils. Oh, yes, there were many who believed that was exactly the case. He drank too. Drank himself into a monster. I always had a holy terror of drunkenness . . . so you see the irony of my own folly? Ha! But your father was my benefactor. He gave me a home.

And she — well, she was perfection as I have said. Perfection and beauty. She was loved . . . And nobody loved her more than I did. She was my life. I was little more than twenty years old. Still a boy really — innocent. Look into your own heart if you want an image of mine . . . But there is a type of man who sees in such perfection nothing but a reproach of his own rottenness. In her presence that man — her monster — began to feel nothing but a deep loathing of himself. What happened was inevitable. Oh Jesus my Saviour, I can't go on with this . . .

OLGA: Oh please, we must.

KUZOVKIN: Other women. Women as dissolute as he was. One in particular. A devil. He started to spend all his time with her. Stayed away for days on end, God forgive him, while your blessed mother sat, not speaking a word, hour after hour, night after night, tears in those radiant angel eyes . . . my heart breaking . . . unable to breathe a word of comfort, I was so in awe of that sweet perfection. My words! They were like clods of earth in my mouth. And there was nobody else to soothe away her bitter sorrow. None of our neighbors would come near his house. She sat there — in the window, her book unopened . . . When I came into this room just now and saw you there, it was her I was seeing — staring at the road through the fields . . . never moving . . . through the sunset, watching the moon rise over the wheat.

What more can I say about her husband? As time went on, he became more and more a stranger to us — cruel, jealous — though the good Lord is our witness he had nothing to be jealous of — but the more your mother put up with his faults the more terrible he became to her. It was as if he was pushing her to see how much she would stand. It was evil. That's the only word, the right word for what he was to her . . . Until, at last he abandoned her entirely. Went to live in town with his devil and left his angel wife to fend for herself. Oh, Olya, dearest Olya, how she suffered? You see, she could not find the way to make herself stop loving him . . . Imagine it . . . Forgive me.

OLGA: For speaking the truth?

KUZOVKIN: How can you bear to hear more of this? After six months he came back. His woman had grown tired of him. We didn't find out until much later. He locked himself in his room. And then . . . he began the long process of humiliation — beatings, yes — but it was more the cruel insults that, at last, started to break her spirit. Hunting and drinking, that's how he spent all his time. What happened then was . . .

OLGA: Go on.

KUZOVKIN: I think . . . How would I truly judge? I know nothing except by feeling — but I think the truth is that her sanity began to fail. She would go into the icon room and stand crossing herself before the holy images. Smiling sometimes. And all the time my heart was aching for her sorrows. She could hardly eat. Nobody spoke to her except me. The servants moved about the house like ghosts. Can you imagine that? That strange unnatural silence. In the evening she would talk to me — in here, this room — and it was all about him . . . until one night, suddenly it was as if her love for him had broken. She turned to me, and looked at me, and after a long, long silence when I could feel my heart beating as though it would explode in my breast — I loved her so hopelessly — and I knew . . . I knew . . . what she was going to say, and oh . . . quite suddenly, and calmly she said: "Vassily Semyonitch. I know how deeply and purely you love me, and I know at last that he has never loved me, and that he will never feel anything for me but contempt and loathing . . . But I feel for you . . . I need . . ." And she laid her head on my breast . . . And, oh Olya! I didn't know what to say or do. We were both lost. Forgive me, please forgive me. I can't tell you any more about it. It's not right that I should.

OLGA: How did he die?

KUZOVKIN: The very next day . . . As soon as it began to grow light I went out into the fields. I remember the skylarks. I was still in a dream. Somebody brought the news — rode over from the next village. Your father had fallen from his horse. They'd carried his body into a priest's house. I watched your mother go off in the carriage. Dear Lord, we thought she would go mad. She was hardly alive herself — right up until the time you were born. And then, as you know, she never recovered — it was as if, for the rest of her life, she inhabited some other, better world. *(He sinks.)*

OLGA: And I . . . I am your daughter. *(She pauses.)* Is there any proof of this?

KUZOVKIN: *(Shaken.)* Merciful God! Proof? Olga Petrovna, I have proof of nothing — there is no proof! That I would dare! Had I not made such a fool of myself yesterday the truth would have gone with me to my grave. I'd sooner have died. Why the good Lord did not strike me down in my folly I shall never know. Until yesterday not a soul . . . I would not even whisper it to my own soul . . . Dear God!

When your father — that man died, I tried to run away, but I was such a coward. It would have been the right thing to do, but I could not leave her, I could not break from her. And then I was afraid. The world out there terrifies me. Poverty, unkindness, the insolence of life. So, God forgive me, I did nothing. Oh, do not mistake me, dear Olya. I did not continue to hope . . . In those days, months after his death I never saw your mother. She locked herself away. She locked her mind — shut out the world. Only Praskovya Ivanova, her maid . . . And later on, and I swear this before God, I was too little of a man to dare to look her in the face. There are no proofs, Olga Petrovna, of anything.

But what were you thinking? That I should dare to use . . . Olga Petrovna, whatever men may say of me, I was born a gentleman and I have tried to honour my birth. I would never, never repeat my folly. Had you not insisted — but please never imagine that you will hear of this again. Nobody will believe the words of a fool and nor should you. Tell yourself that it's all lies, the ramblings of a man losing his mind. Make that your truth.

OLGA: No. Vassily Semyonitch . . . I believe every word you have spoken.

KUZOVKIN: You believe me . . .

OLGA: Yes. And it's a truth that may destroy us all. What can I be sure of now? My husband, my home? I don't even know who I am.

KUZOVKIN: Oh. Olga Petrovna you must not think of it . . . I'm not an evil man. I have tried to show you what I did — why I — only because you . . . Do you not guess how much I have loved you? How much I will always love you? I am not a fool, after all . . . You see, you are . . . you are my . . . *(He gets up quickly.)* There's nothing to fear. I'll go at once. You'll hear no more of me. Forgive what I have done. I shall pray for you always. I have thrown away my last hope of happiness. *(He weeps.)*

OLGA: *Please don't . . .*

KUZOVKIN: *(Holding out his hands.)* Good-bye.

(Olga runs into her study.)

KUZOVKIN: *My God, my God!*

FOUR
Christopher Shinn

Dexter is nineteen. He's a low-level drug dealer, out on a date with Abigayle. She's sixteen.

In Dexter's car. Driving. Dexter is nineteen, half Puerto Rican, half white, wearing baggy jeans, a T-shirt, and a baseball cap. Abigayle sits next to him, looking out the window.

DEXTER: I don't know about all that, you know. All that food. It was getting to be too much. But I didn't know anything. I mean, my aunt, my aunt was there, and she was like all telling me how I'd grown and shit. So. You know.

ABIGAYLE: What in God's green earth are you talking about?

DEXTER: I don't know. So uhm — why'd you change your mind?

ABIGAYLE: Can't I just change my mind?

DEXTER: There's gotta be a reason, right? You change your mind, something happens, right?

ABIGAYLE: I just changed my mind. No reason.

DEXTER: Always a reason. I always went to church on Sunday with everybody and then I stopped going to church 'cuz I changed my mind.

ABIGAYLE: And why'd you do that? *(Beat. Dexter tries to think.)* So you can get off this subject now.

DEXTER: No, I know why, I'm just trying to figure out how to ar-tic-u-late it.

ABIGAYLE: Mmm-hmmm.

DEXTER: Damn. You gonna be all bitchy. I don't wanna be with you. I'll take you *home.*

ABIGAYLE: You'll take me however I am. And don't call me a bitch.

DEXTER: I didn't call you a bitch.

ABIGAYLE: Yes you did.

DEXTER: I said you were acting bitchy. I didn't call you a bitch. I never call a woman a bitch.

ABIGAYLE: You call your mother a bitch.

DEXTER: She's my mother!

ABIGAYLE: Mmmm-hmmmm. *(A beat.)*

DEXTER: All right. Starting over. Commercial break. Lah de dah. Where you wanna go?

ABIGAYLE: I dunno. Where is there to go?

DEXTER: The park.

ABIGAYLE: I don't like the park.

DEXTER: Then where? You don't wanna see the fireworks, you don't wanna go to the park. You don't wanna go nowhere.

ABIGAYLE: I don't like anywhere. I hate this town.

DEXTER: Why?

ABIGAYLE: There's nothing here but *town.* Even the city. It's not even a city. Nothing happens here.

DEXTER: Mark Twain lived here.

ABIGAYLE: Nine thousand years ago.

DEXTER: There's stuff. The Hartford Whalers.

ABIGAYLE: You like hockey?

DEXTER: No. So we'll just drive then. Drive around. That's fun.

ABIGAYLE: Let's drive to New York.

DEXTER: New York? That's two hours!

ABIGAYLE: I was just kidding. Dag.

DEXTER: Oh.

ABIGAYLE: It would be fun if you had a convertible. That would be fun.

DEXTER: *(Beat.)* Hey uhhh — I was thinking of something.

ABIGAYLE: What?

DEXTER: Your story. About the movie.

ABIGAYLE: Yeah?

DEXTER: Made me remember something myself.

ABIGAYLE: What'd it make you remember?

DEXTER: Made me remember my first trip to McDonald's.

ABIGAYLE: Your first trip to *McDonald's?*

DEXTER: Yeah. Why you say it like that?

ABIGAYLE: Go, tell your story.

DEXTER: *(In a vaguely performance-like tone.)* Well, I was remembering that
I had wanted to go to McDonald's for a while, 'cuz my friend Chris
Taylor had his *birthday* party when he was *six years old* at McDon-
ald's, but I didn't become *friends* with him until *after* he turned *six* —

ABIGAYLE: Can you just talk normal?

DEXTER: What? What'd I do?

ABIGAYLE: Just talk normal.

DEXTER: I talk how I talk. How do I talk?

ABIGAYLE: I'm sorry. Keep going.

DEXTER: So, what I was saying was, *Chris* Taylor would not stop *talking*
about how *great* McDonald's was, how he had *McNuggets* and all this
shit, and *orange drink,* and *fries,* and a *sundae,* and how Ronald *Mc-
Donald* was there, and shit, so I was excited, right? And every time
home from school the bus would go in front of McDonald's. Now
I asked my mother to take me to McDonald's, but she said she didn't
have any *money,* which was bullshit because she was always buying
crossword puzzle magazines and *Vaseline* for her lips, so I knew she
had money, there was just some *reason* she didn't want to go to Mc-
Donald's. So I went to McDonald's myself. I *walked* home from
school, *to* the McDonald's, and I was *scared,* walking in there, never
having been there before, having all that excitement and butterflies
in my stomach like before when I play a game —

ABIGAYLE: — Don't start bragging about your basketball skills —

DEXTER: I didn't!

ABIGAYLE: Don't start!

DEXTER: Chill! All right, *so,* I get into the McDonald's — and I go up in
the line, and this guy, big brother nine feet tall —

ABIGAYLE: You're not black, he's not a brother.

DEXTER: I grew up with black people!

ABIGAYLE: Keep going, tell the story.

DEXTER: I look up at the *menu,* way up high, I look up at the *menu* and
I realize — shit, I can't read. I can't read nothing but, like, Dick and
Jane, and shit. I don't know *shit* about what they got at McDonald's.
All I remember is the *commercial.* The Big Mac *commercial* and the
chicken *McNuggets* and the *orange drink* and the *sundae* and the *fries*
'cuz Chris Taylor was always talking about what he ate. So I stand

there all scared and I say, "I'll have a Big Mac, a Chicken McNuggets, an orange drink, fries, and a sundae. "Ain't that fucking funny?!

ABIGAYLE: Where'd you get all that money?

DEXTER: Hunh?

ABIGAYLE: That's a lot of money.

Dexter. I took it.

ABIGAYLE: From who?

DEXTER: I don't remember. I just took it.

ABIGAYLE: You just made up that story.

DEXTER: I did not!

ABIGAYLE: Yes you did. Where'd you get that money?

DEXTER: I don't remember! So! Anyway, the story ends . . . you know, I paid and I sat down and I ate all the food and I thought it was GREAT, the best MMMMMMM just the best fucking food *ever*, right? But I had basketball after that. Basketball at South Catholic. I went there and I started playing and then I started feeling like a big lump was in my belly or something, and I threw up all over the court, and the shit was, you could *see* the chunks of chicken and the fries and shit, it was *nasty*, and everyone made fun of me like, you just threw up you jerk, and my mom was like where the *hell* did you eat that shit? Yeah. Yeah. So — that's the end.

ABIGAYLE: Oh.

DEXTER: What?

ABIGAYLE: Nothing.

DEXTER: You not impressed by my story?

ABIGAYLE: Your story's good. It's a good story.

DEXTER: My dad used to work at McDonald's, dat's where my mom met him and shit. *(A beat.) I* made up that last part. I didn't throw up. I just kept burping a lot. *(Abigayle smiles. Dexter shrugs cutely.)* So where you wanna go?

ABIGAYLE: Go to South Catholic.

DEXTER: Hunh?

ABIGAYLE: Go to South Catholic.

DEXTER: Why you wanna go there?

ABIGAYLE: Where do you want to go? *(Dexter has no answer. Blackout.)*

GOLDEN LADDER
Donna Spector

Aaron and Catherine are two teenagers. Aaron is Jewish. Catherine has been told by her friend Mary that Jewish boys are really hot to trot.

AARON: I hear it's your birthday.

CATHERINE: Y'know, maybe you've got the wrong idea.

AARON: It's not your birthday?

CATHERINE: Well, it is, but . . .

AARON: Your fourteenth?

CATHERINE: I don't know what you've heard about me, y'know, but . . .

AARON: Well, I heard you're very smart. Y'know. Best grades in your class. And, uh, well . . . You write poems. No, I didn't *hear* that, really. I read them. They're good.

CATHERINE: How do you know?

AARON: I guess it's just my opinion. I'm not a poet.

CATHERINE: You're a math person.

AARON: Yeah. Well. Uh, that's not all I am.

CATHERINE: Oh, I know.

AARON: there is no canopy
    for hiding, my love
    I have prepared
    a horse for riding
    time is open now
    let your body glisten
    in the sun

CATHERINE: That's my poem!

AARON: Yes.

CATHERINE: How did you remember it?

AARON: *(He continues to quote.)* who sings his song
    in our heart
    let him sing

to the sun
for we have chased
the horses of the moon away
and we hold the light
in our hands

CATHERINE: I can't believe you know it. *(Beat.)* So, uh . . . How old are you?

AARON: Fifteen.

CATHERINE: That means at least two more. Maybe two and a half.

AARON: What?

CATHERINE: So, where do we, y'know, *go?*

AARON: What do you mean?

(Stares at her breasts.)

You look different. From when I saw you yesterday.

CATHERINE: *(Crossing her arms over her chest.)* You think so?

AARON: Yes. *(Beat.)* You want to *go* somewhere?

CATHERINE: Well, sure. I mean. We can't just stay here.

AARON: We can't?

CATHERINE: Well, I *mean. (Beat.)* Maybe it's not really true, what they say.

AARON: What do they say?

CATHERINE: You know.

AARON: I don't. *(Beat.)* You're really pretty up close.

CATHERINE: I'm not pretty.

AARON: Yes, you are. You're very pretty. *(Beat.)* Want to go swimming?

CATHERINE: In the *pool?*

AARON: You know anywhere else we could go swimming?

CATHERINE: No, I meant . . . I don't know very much, even though I'm fourteen. But the *pool? (Beat.)*

How'd you find out about me?

AARON: Well, I . . . Y'know, I . . . Oh, maybe . . . *(Deep breath.)* I just saw you, and I knew.

CATHERINE: I figured.

AARON: Y'know, I . . . Well . . . I'd been watching you a long time.

CATHERINE: Waiting.

AARON: Well, sort of. I mean, it's hard, y'know.

CATHERINE: Is it? Okay. I guess I have to know. You just can't escape your destiny.

AARON: Are you my destiny? Is that what you think? I mean . . .

CATHERINE: It looks like it.

AARON: Can I . . . ? What do you think? Could I . . . kiss you then?

CATHERINE: I suppose.

(*They kiss tentatively.*)

AARON: You're Jewish, aren't you?

CATHERINE: (*To audience.*) Then I knew. It showed. (*To Aaron.*) Not really.

AARON: What do you mean?

CATHERINE: Well, my mother's not Jewish, and my father was *born* Jewish, but . . .

AARON: Oh, I see what you mean. It's like a maternal lineage.

CATHERINE: What?

AARON: You know. Jews say you have to have a Jewish mother to be really Jewish.

CATHERINE: Really? Then I'm not Jewish?

AARON: Why? You don't want to be Jewish?

CATHERINE: No, it's not that. (*Beat.*) I just worry about the Jewish hormones.

AARON: Jewish hormones?

CATHERINE: Hormones are in the blood, aren't they?

AARON: Are they?

CATHERINE: So if my father was born Jewish, then he has Jewish blood, and I have some too, so I must have Jewish hormones.

AARON: This is the weirdest conversation.

CATHERINE: In which case, I'll probably end up doing it.

AARON: What?

CATHERINE: Going all the way.

AARON: I beg your pardon?

CATHERINE: But if my father quit being Jewish to be an atheist and my mother says being Jewish is a religion, not, y'know, something cultural . . .

AARON: It's both.

CATHERINE: Oh. Hell. Then I guess I'll have to do it. With you.

AARON: Oh. *(Beat.)* You . . . I mean . . . You're not the person I thought you were.

CATHERINE: What did you think?

AARON: Uh, y'know . . . You're really fast.

CATHERINE: I guess I am. I tried not to be, but . . .

AARON: I mean, most girls don't start talking about going all the way with a boy they just met.

CATHERINE: I've had no experience talking to boys. I didn't know.

AARON: You mean you just do it and don't talk?

CATHERINE: I never did, but . . .

AARON: Wow. Maybe we should go over to my house. There's nobody home.

CATHERINE: Okay.

AARON: *(Takes her hand as they start walking off.)* Total silence. Hunh.

CATHERINE: *(Stops and speaks to audience.)* We went to his house and we tried to do it. We fumbled around a while, very embarrassed but not speaking. *(To Aaron.)* You don't know *anything*.

AARON: Gee, thanks. You don't know anything either.

CATHERINE: Well, I don't have to. I just turned fourteen.

AARON: So what was all this about going all the way?

CATHERINE: You ought to know. Didn't you start when you were ten?

AARON: Sex? When I was ten?

CATHERINE: I thought you'd done it with like twelve or so girls by now.

AARON: Shit! You did?

CATHERINE: Sure. What about your hormones?

AARON: What is this crap about hormones?

CATHERINE: Mary told me if you're Jewish, you've got more hormones, and you've got to go all the way with girls by the time you're four-teen.

AARON: I can't believe she said that.

CATHERINE: And she said you'd gone all the way with ten girls by last year.

AARON: Cathy. Don't you ever question things your friends say?

CATHERINE: She said she read it in *Seventeen*.

AARON: *Seventeen.* The ultimate medical and scientific authority. *(He starts laughing.)* That is so funny! Y'know, you ought to write a story about this.

CATHERINE: I don't think it's very funny.

AARON: Well, it is. Extra hormones.

(Aaron laughs even harder.)

CATHERINE: I'm going home.

AARON: Wait. I'm sorry. I'm not really laughing at you. Well, I am, sort of, but not in a mean way.

CATHERINE: I'm grateful to you for enlightening me. But I'd like to leave now.

AARON: Oh, Cathy. Couldn't we be friends?

CATHERINE: I don't think so. You make me feel stupid.

AARON: You're not stupid. Maybe, y'know, a little naïve, but that's okay.

CATHERINE: It's not okay.

AARON: It's okay with me. Could I kiss you?

CATHERINE: No.

AARON: Just a friendly kiss. *(Beat.)* I'll tell you the truth. You're the first girl I've ever kissed.

CATHERINE: Not even a kiss?

AARON: Not even one. Till you.

CATHERINE: You're the first boy I ever kissed.

AARON: I know.

CATHERINE: Okay, then.

(She raises her face. He bends down to meet her. They kiss, carefully, then more prolonged.)

CATHERINE: Oh. I think that's probably enough.

AARON: Why?

CATHERINE: *(She backs away from him. Both are breathless.)* Because I feel you down there, and it makes me nervous.

AARON: Okay. Okay. I don't want to make you nervous.

CATHERINE: I'll be your friend, Aaron. Even if we don't have extra hormones.

(They both start laughing uncontrollably.)

GOOD THING
Jessica Goldberg

Liz and Dean are both in their twenties. They were once an item, but Dean has married Someone Else. This scene takes place in Liz's bedroom, where they have just had sex.

Liz's bedroom. Liz and Dean are in bed; they did it; her hand rests on his chest. They smile to themselves in the darkness.

LIZ: So, now we did it.

DEAN: Yuhp.

LIZ: Nice.

DEAN: Yeah.

LIZ: You still have your boots on. I hate that.

DEAN: Happens to you a lot?

LIZ: What's that, married man?

DEAN: Ugh, very bad kids, both of us.

LIZ: Yeah . . . but not really bad . . .

DEAN: No.

LIZ: It's worse to let things get built up in your head, better to . . . you know.

DEAN: So we could stop wondering —

DEAN AND LIZ: Right, right.

LIZ: Get it out of our system —

DEAN: Years of —

LIZ: It had to happen already.

DEAN: Now it's done.

LIZ: We can move on. *(Quiet.)* Do you love her?

DEAN: What?

LIZ: How long have you been married?

DEAN: Seven months. *(Beat.)*

LIZ: So uhmmm . . . Can I remove your boots?

DEAN: I should sort of go.

LIZ: Oh.

> *(Dean gets up, suddenly seized with guilt and desperate to get out; his pants and shoes are still on, wrapped around his ankles. He pulls them up, starts rummaging through the bed for his shirt.)*

LIZ: What do you do these days? You still read a lot?

DEAN: Yeah, read, work, work a lot mostly.

LIZ: Still listen to music?

DEAN: *(Looking for his shirt.)* Yeah, well, you know . . .

LIZ: I think about all the books and music and stuff you exposed me to, it prepared me for college more than high school did. *(Dean nods.)*

DEAN: Have you seen my shirt?

LIZ: I was studying to be, get this, a doctor.

DEAN: That's great. My shirt?

LIZ: Don't you think that's weird?

DEAN: What?

LIZ: Me, a doctor?

DEAN: Not really.

LIZ: I do.

DEAN: Why? It makes sense.

LIZ: What? You really could see me as a doctor?

DEAN: Look, Liz, I've got responsibilities.

LIZ: Oh, yeah, like cheating on your wife? *(Dean's getting mad, confused; there's a slight noise coming through the wall.)*

DEAN: I have never cheated on my wife . . . before, and this, fuck you, this was — just please I really want to find my shirt, will you help, please, find my shirt.

LIZ: Maybe it's in your boots!

DEAN: Thanks a lot — what's that? *(He listens, she listens, the sound of heavy breathing, moaning . . .)* What's that noise?

LIZ: My mom.

DEAN: Your mom is fucking fucking, holy shit, your mom is getting off.

LIZ: Shut up.

DEAN: Holy fuck, man, that is so intense, listen to her.

LIZ: Stop.

DEAN: I can't believe her room is right next to yours, she is a wild woman —

LIZ: Stop!

DEAN: That is so fucked up, mother and daughter going at it —

LIZ: Stop it!

DEAN: Hah!

LIZ: *(Over the following, the moans peter out and become quiet.)* Stop it! Stop it! She's such a fucking cunt with her stupid boyfriends and they're not even boyfriends, they don't even like her, she's just a miserable, miserable person with no, no . . . values, just, just this, this sponge of her own needs, and, and needs and, and I think I'm better, not better, nohoho! Stupid, ugly shit, just like her.

DEAN: *(Reaching to her.)* Liz —

(She slaps his hand away.)

LIZ: That's why I came home you asshole, 'cause the only time I was happy, just myself, was with you! All those long stupid nights talking reading poetry bullshit with you, being a loser with you. *(She cries.)*

DEAN: *(Scared.)* Don't . . . cry.

(Liz buries her face in her hands, weeps. Dean sits on the floor at the foot of the bed, at a loss. [. . .])

DEAN: Sometimes I thought if you told me you were leaving, maybe I would've . . . *(Liz looks up at him.)* I coulda. I didn't do so bad in school, I could've done really well if I didn't have such an attitude problem. I aced the S.A.T.'s. Sometimes I fantasized I went with you to Ithaca — wherever, we'd be in your dorm room, studying on your bed, covered in books . . . we'd be working on some paper like about Jean-Paul Sartre's philosophy of . . . *(Gestures "whatever.")*

LIZ: *Being and Nothingness.*

DEAN: Whatever, I didn't know what I was talking about, shit, I don't even know who the fuck Jean-Paul Sartre is.

LIZ: He was a French philosopher, he had —

DEAN: Oh, please don't tell me.

(Liz smiles, a beat.)

LIZ: You would've hated school anyway. It's sort of like a factory: You enter this teenager, all like, who the hell am I? Four years later they pop you out and you don't have to worry about who you are anymore, because you're like an English major or a business major or pre-med. So even if you like work in 7-Eleven for the rest of your life you can be like, "Yeah, I work in 7-Eleven, but I'm really an English major. *(They laugh.)* There was no one at school better than you. I just wish I had known that before . . .

DEAN: Well, we all gotta learn however we learn, right?

LIZ: Well, I gotta learn faster then, if I keep going like this everything'll be gone by the time I figure it out. Three years of college to learn that this, you . . . that I had to get back to you as soon as possible and . . .

DEAN: Take on the world together?

LIZ: Yeah!

DEAN: Hey, no regrets, right?

    (Liz nods.)

DEAN: Shit . . . Please, please just go back to school, okay?

    (They look at each other, come together, begin to kiss again, getting heavy into each other. Suddenly, she slaps him away. The moans have started again, softly.)

Liz: *Oh my god! I can't fucking believe her!*

DEAN: *(Weak.)* She's doing it again?

LIZ: She wants to destroy my last shreds of dignity — let's go to your house.

DEAN: What? *(She stands.)*

LIZ: *I'm not going to say anything.*

DEAN: You can't.

LIZ: *(Getting hysterical again.)* I can't think in this house. I need to think. I just —

DEAN: But —

LIZ: If you care about me even the slightest —

DEAN: I do, but uhmm. Liz, uhm —

LIZ: Look, I'm not gonna destroy your perfect little marriage, if you ever had any feelings for me at all —

DEAN: I do, yes, but she's really pregnant and —

LIZ: Look, I just fucked you and I want to go to your house! *(The moans intensify.)* Ughhh! Let's go!! *(Liz storms out the door.)*

DEAN: My shirt? *(Dean picks up his jacket from the floor and runs after her.)*

THE GRADUATE

Terry Johnson

This is, indeed, a stage version of the Mike Nichols film. In this scene, Benjamin, twenties, a recent college graduate, confronts Elaine, twenties, a young woman he was dating until she found out he was having an affair with her mother (the legendary Mrs. Robinson). Benjamin's life since college has been nothing but confusion. Now, he knows what he wants. He wants Elaine.

Attic room, Berkeley Boarding House. Evening. Benjamin stands holding the door open for Elaine.

ELAINE: Benjamin, why are you here?

BENJAMIN: Would you like to come in?

ELAINE: I want to know what you're doing here in Berkeley.

BENJAMIN: Would you like some tea? I have tea.

ELAINE: I want to know why you're stalking me.

BENJAMIN: I'm not.

ELAINE: I see you on campus. You duck into doorways. On the bus you hid behind a magazine.

BENJAMIN: I've been meaning to speak to you.

ELAINE: You've been following me around for days.

BENJAMIN: Would you like to come in?

ELAINE: No!

BENJAMIN: Why not?

ELAINE: I don't want to be in a room with you. Now why are you up here?

BENJAMIN: I'm just living here temporarily. I thought I might be bumping into you. I thought I remembered you were going to school up here.

ELAINE: Did you move up here because of me?

BENJAMIN: No.

ELAINE: Did you?

BENJAMIN: I don't know.

ELAINE: Well, did you?

BENJAMIN: Well, what do you think?

ELAINE: I think you did.

BENJAMIN: I'm just living in Berkeley. Having grown somewhat weary of family life, I've been meaning to stop by and pay my respects but have not been entirely certain how you felt about me after the incident with your mother which was certainly a serious mistake on my part but not serious enough I hope to permanently alter your feelings about me.

(Elaine comes in, slamming the door.)

ELAINE: Benjamin, you are the one person in the entire world I never want to see again. I want you nowhere near me. I want you to leave here and never come back.

(He hangs his head.)

ELAINE: Promise me you'll go.

BENJAMIN: Elaine . . .

ELAINE: Promise me.

BENJAMIN: *(He stares at her a moment.)* Alright.

ELAINE: Pack your bags and go tonight.

BENJAMIN: Alright!

ELAINE: So promise me.

BENJAMIN: Alright!

(He flops down, his head in his arms.)

ELAINE: Good-bye, Benjamin.

BENJAMIN: I love you.

ELAINE: You what?

BENJAMIN: I love you. I love you and I can't help myself and I'm begging you to forgive me for what I did. I love you so much I'm terrified of seeing you every time I step outside the door I feel helpless and hopeless and lost and miserable, please forget what I did please Elaine o god Elaine I love you please forget what I did? Please forget what I did Elaine. I love you.

ELAINE: Yeah, well, I don't think so.

BENJAMIN: I do.

ELAINE: You do not.

BENJAMIN: Honestly, I . . .

ELAINE: How can you love me Benjamin when you're so full of hate?

BENJAMIN: Of hate?

ELAINE: How else could you have done that?

BENJAMIN: Done what?

ELAINE: How could you have raped my mother?

BENJAMIN: What?

ELAINE: You must have so much hate inside you.

BENJAMIN: Raped her?

(Elaine starts to cry.)

BENJAMIN: Did you say raped her?

ELAINE: Virtually raped her.

BENJAMIN: Did she say that?

ELAINE: I want you out of here by the morning.

BENJAMIN: No!

(He runs between her and the door.)

ELAINE: Don't you touch me.

BENJAMIN: I'm not.

ELAINE: Then get away from the door.

BENJAMIN: What did she say? What did she say?

ELAINE: Why?

BENJAMIN: Because it isn't true.

ELAINE: She said you virtually raped her.

BENJAMIN: Which isn't true.

ELAINE: Is it true you slept with her?

BENJAMIN: Yes.

ELAINE: All right then, get away from the door.

BENJAMIN: What did she say? What did she say?

ELAINE: She said you dragged her up to the hotel room . . .

BENJAMIN: I dragged her?!

ELAINE: . . . and you made her pass out and you raped her.

BENJAMIN: I what I drugged her? I dragged her up five floors and I drugged her? I raped her?

ELAINE: You *virtually*, yes.

BENJAMIN: I *what?*

ELAINE: Could I leave now please?

BENJAMIN: That is not what happened.

ELAINE: I have to leave.

BENJAMIN: My parents gave me a party when I got home from college. Your mother came up to my room.

ELAINE: I don't want to hear this.

BENJAMIN: She asked me to unzip her dress.

ELAINE: May I go now?

BENJAMIN: She took off all her clothes. She stood there entirely naked and she said . . .

(Elaine screams, long and hysterical. Benjamin frozen. She calms down. He brings her a chair. He brings her a glass of water. She drinks it.)

ELAINE: What did you think would happen?

BENJAMIN: What?

ELAINE: When you came up here?

BENJAMIN: I drove up. I made reservations at a restaurant.

ELAINE: You were going to invite me to dinner?

BENJAMIN: Yes.

ELAINE: Then what did you do?

BENJAMIN: I didn't invite you.

ELAINE: I know.

BENJAMIN: I just came up here. I got this room. I kind of wallowed around. I wrote you some letters.

ELAINE: Love letters?

BENJAMIN: I don't remember.

ELAINE: So what are you going to do now?

BENJAMIN: I don't know.

ELAINE: Where are you going?

BENJAMIN: I don't know.

ELAINE: Well what are you going to do?

BENJAMIN: Are you deaf?

ELAINE: Excuse me?

BENJAMIN: I don't know what I'm going to do.

ELAINE: Well, will you get on a bus or what?

BENJAMIN: Are you concerned about me or something?

ELAINE: You came up here because of me. You messed up your life because of me, and now you're leaving because of me. You made me responsible! I don't want you drunk in some gutter because of me.

BENJAMIN: You want me to stick around?

ELAINE: I want you to have a definite plan before you leave, then I want you to leave.

BENJAMIN: I have no plans.

ELAINE: Then just make up your mind.

BENJAMIN: What?

ELAINE: Don't you have a mind?

BENJAMIN: Of course.

ELAINE: Then make it up.

BENJAMIN: I could go to Canada.

ELAINE: You want to go to Canada?

BENJAMIN: No.

ELAINE: You think I can study? You think I can think with you here?

BENJAMIN: Just tell me to leave and I'll leave.

ELAINE: I have so much work to do this semester.

BENJAMIN: Would you just tell me to leave, please?

ELAINE: Are you simple?

BENJAMIN: What?

ELAINE: I mean what do I have to say to you?

BENJAMIN: I don't know.

ELAINE: Can't you see the way I feel?

BENJAMIN: Shall I go then?

ELAINE: Why don't you.

BENJAMIN: Why don't I go?

ELAINE: Yes.

BENJAMIN: Alright. That's all you had to say.

(Elaine goes to the door.)

ELAINE: You know what she gave me for my eleventh birthday? She game me a Bartender's Guide. I made her cocktails all day.

BENJAMIN: She's a strange woman.

ELAINE: Is she attractive?

BENJAMIN: Yes. Not really.

ELAINE: Well is she or not?

BENJAMIN: I don't know.

ELAINE: You don't know which she is or you don't know which I'd like to hear?

BENJAMIN: Either.

ELAINE: And am I?

BENJAMIN: I'm sorry?

ELAINE: Am I as attractive as her?

BENJAMIN: Oh, yes.

ELAINE: I have to go now.

BENJAMIN: Would you marry me?

ELAINE: Would I what?

BENJAMIN: Marry me. Would you?

ELAINE: Marry you?

BENJAMIN: Yes.

ELAINE: Marry you?

BENJAMIN: Would you?

ELAINE: Why would I?

BENJAMIN: I think we have a lot in common.

ELAINE: Well, that's true.

BENJAMIN: So will you?

ELAINE: Marry you?

BENJAMIN: Yes.

ELAINE: Hah. Ha ha ha. Oh Benjamin, you are something.

BENJAMIN: Am I?

ELAINE: Yes you are, but I don't know what. Why do you want to marry me?

BENJAMIN: It's the way I feel. I feel we should.

ELAINE: What about the way I feel?

BENJAMIN: How do you feel?

ELAINE: Confused.

BENJAMIN: Are you fond of me?

(She sniffs.)

BENJAMIN: Are you?

ELAINE: Yes, fond.

BENJAMIN: Then let's get married.

ELAINE: And can you imagine my parents?

BENJAMIN: You mean your mother?

ELAINE: I mean my father.

BENJAMIN: I think he'd be very happy for us.

ELAINE: And what if he found out what happened?

BENJAMIN: He won't.

ELAINE: But what if he did?

BENJAMIN: I'd apologize. I'd say it was a stupid foolish thing and he'd say he was a little disappointed in me but if it's all in the past then, that's that.

ELAINE: You are so naïve.

BENJAMIN: Forget about your parents. This isn't about our parents. This is about us. Have you any other objections?

ELAINE: Yes I do.

BENJAMIN: What are they?

ELAINE: We're too young to be married. You should do other things first.

BENJAMIN: What other things?

ELAINE: Well, go somewhere. Asia. Africa. See different places, different people.

BENJAMIN: Elaine, I have no desire to hop around the world ogling peasants. So do you have any other objections?

ELAINE: Have you thought about finding a place to live and buying the groceries every day?

BENJAMIN: Sure.

ELAINE: No you haven't.

BENJAMIN: You mean which brand of cereal we should buy?

ELAINE: Yes.

BENJAMIN: No I haven't.

ELAINE: Well why not? I mean, that's the kind of thing you'll have to be thinking about, Benjamin, and I think you'd get sick of it after two days.

BENJAMIN: But I wouldn't get sick of you, would I?

ELAINE: Well yes, I think you probably would.

BENJAMIN: Well no, I wouldn't.

ELAINE: I'm not what you think I am, Benjamin. I'm just a plain ordinary person. I'm not smart or glamorous or anything like that.

BENJAMIN: So what?

ELAINE: Well . . . So why me?

BENJAMIN: Well. You're reasonably intelligent. You're striking looking.

ELAINE: Striking?

BENJAMIN: Sure.

ELAINE: My ears are too prominent to be striking looking.

BENJAMIN: No, they're very striking.

ELAINE: I wouldn't be enough for you, Benjamin.

BENJAMIN: That isn't true.

ELAINE: You're an intellectual, and I'm not.

BENJAMIN: Now listen . . .

ELAINE: You should marry someone who can discuss politics and history and art . . .

BENJAMIN: Ah, shut up.

ELAINE: Excuse me?

BENJAMIN: Would you just . . . thank you. Now have you ever heard me talking about any of that crap?

ELAINE: You majored in that crap.

BENJAMIN: Have you ever heard me talk about it?

ELAINE: That crap?

BENJAMIN: Yes.

ELAINE: No I haven't.

BENJAMIN: All right then. Goddammit, I hate all that. So will you marry me?

ELAINE: No!

BENJAMIN: Why not?

ELAINE: Well for a start I'm studying and you haven't got any money!

BENJAMIN: I'll move up here. I'll get a job teaching.

ELAINE: I thought you didn't want to be a teacher.

BENJAMIN: Yes, but I could teach.

ELAINE: You don't have the right attitude. Teachers are meant to be inspired.

BENJAMIN: That's a myth.

ELAINE: Is it?

BENJAMIN: Oh yeh.

ELAINE: It is not.

BENJAMIN: Any other objections?

ELAINE: Plenty.

BENJAMIN: Take your best shot.

ELAINE: Well, what about babies.

BENJAMIN: Babies?

ELAINE: Do you want babies? Because that's what I want.

BENJAMIN: Well, I do too.

ELAINE: Oh, come on.

BENJAMIN: I do.

ELAINE: You do not.

BENJAMIN: Goddammit Elaine I want babies! Your babies! Triplets! I want to smother in a huge pile of diapers!

(She laughs.)

BENJAMIN: I'm serious here. Let's get married.

ELAINE: Benjamin.

BENJAMIN: What?

ELAINE: I can't see why I'm so attractive to you.

BENJAMIN: You just are.

ELAINE: But . . . I don't understand.

BENJAMIN: What don't you understand?

ELAINE: I mean you're a really brilliant person.

BENJAMIN: Elaine, don't start that. I mean it.

(She nods. He takes her hand.)

BENJAMIN: So, shall we get married?

ELAINE: Benjamin! If you want to marry me so much why don't you just . . . drag me off.

BENJAMIN: Alright, I will. We'll get a blood test in the morning and I'll just drag you off.

ELAINE: But you can't. I mean I couldn't. Besides I'd have to see Carl.

BENJAMIN: Carl?

ELAINE: I'd have to talk to Carl first.

BENJAMIN: Who's Carl?

ELAINE: The boy I met last semester. Carl Smith.

BENJAMIN: Well, what does he have to do with it?

ELAINE: I said I might marry him.

BENJAMIN: What?

ELAINE: He asked me to marry him and I said I might.

BENJAMIN: Well, Elaine . . .

ELAINE: What?

BENJAMIN: Why in the hell didn't you tell me about this?

ELAINE: I'm telling you.

BENJAMIN: Now? You're telling me now?

ELAINE: Well there wasn't a before. It was none of your business before.

BENJAMIN: My God Elaine, how many people have done this?

ELAINE: Proposed to me?

BENJAMIN: Yes.

ELAINE: I don't know.

BENJAMIN: You mean more than him have?

ELAINE: Well, yes.

BENJAMIN: How many ?

ELAINE: I don't know.

BENJAMIN: Well, could you try and remember? Six? Seven?

ELAINE: About that, yes.

BENJAMIN: Are you kidding me?

ELAINE: No.

BENJAMIN: You mean you have actually had six or seven people ask you
to marry them?

ELAINE: Is this any of your business?

BENJAMIN: Well yes, I think it is. When did he ask you? Was it him on
the bus?

ELAINE: What bus?

BENJAMIN: On the bus to the zoo?

ELAINE: You followed me to the zoo?

BENJAMIN: No. I missed the bus! When did he ask you? Did he ask you
that day? My God, he asked you that day, didn't he? Where did he
ask you, did he ask you at the zoo?

ELAINE: Benjamin, why are you getting so excited?

BENJAMIN: He asked you at the zoo. I missed the bus and he asked you
in the monkey house or somewhere. Did he get down on his knees?
I hope he didn't get down on his knees. He did, didn't he. What did
he say?

ELAINE: Benjamin . . .

BENJAMIN: What did he say?

ELAINE: He said he thought we'd make a pretty good team.

BENJAMIN: Hah!

ELAINE: What?

BENJAMIN: He said that?

ELAINE: Benjamin, what is wrong with you?

BENJAMIN: So what is he, a student?

ELAINE: A medical student. Final year.

BENJAMIN: And he got down on his knees at the zoo and he said . . .

ELAINE: It wasn't at the zoo. It was at his apartment.

BENJAMIN: His apartment?

ELAINE: Yes.

BENJAMIN: You went to his apartment?

ELAINE: Yes.

BENJAMIN: But you . . . I mean you didn't . . . ?

ELAINE: No, I did not spend the night.

(Benjamin grins.)

BENJAMIN: So good old Carl the final year medic took you up to his apartment and popped the big one, did he . . . ?

ELAINE: Good-bye Benjamin.

BENJAMIN: Did he put music on?

ELAINE: I have to study.

BENJAMIN: No wait. Wait. Are we getting a blood test tomorrow?

ELAINE: No.

BENJAMIN: The day after?

ELAINE: I don't know.

BENJAMIN: Are we getting married?

ELAINE: Maybe we are and maybe we aren't.

(She leaves, closing the door behind her. Benjamin sits. Suddenly the door opens, Elaine walks in, kisses him hard, and waltzes out again. Benjamin grins.)

LAST CALL
Kelly McAllister

In this scene, late at night on the anniversary of Sheila's death, Jack sneaks into the bar he and Sheila used to frequent. Much to Jack's surprise, Sheila is there and has no recollection of dying. Jack is in his early thirties, psychologically damaged since his early twenties, and thus very childlike in his mannerisms. He is innocent, kind, trusting. Sheila, just turned twenty-one. She was an art student, full of life, always looking for the next subject to paint, the next song to dance to, the next exciting facet of life to explore. As a ghost, she doesn't realize she is dead.

> *A dark, empty bar in Salinas, California. There are a few empty tables and chairs, a jukebox, and one door to the outside. It is about ten minutes before dawn. Sheila, a pretty young woman, twenty-one, is sitting at a booth. She is the only person in the bar. A noise is heard from the back area of the bar. Sheila smiles. Jack cautiously walks in. Jack is in his early thirties. He has a somewhat frumpy appearance. Jack doesn't see Sheila. A wolf is heard howling in the distance. Jack is scared by the howl at first, then smiles in recognition. He walks to the back of the bar and puts money in the jukebox. The song "Lights" by Journey starts to play. Jack begins to dance to the music, play air guitar, and sing along.*

SHEILA: *(Loud enough for Jack to hear over the music.)* Nice butt!

JACK: *(Freezes. Slowly turns around.)* Hello?

SHEILA: *(Taking out a pencil and sketch pad.)* Don't move, I want to catch those buns.

JACK: Who's there?

SHEILA: I'll give you a hint. I'm a red hot, groovy sex kitten, and I love tomatoes and Chinese cooking.

JACK: Sheila?

SHEILA: In the flesh.

JACK: Sheila! Jesus, you scared me. *(Goes to light switch, turns on lights.)*

SHEILA: *(Rising.)* Wanna dance?

JACK: What are you doing here?

(She goes to Jack, puts her hands around his neck.)

SHEILA: You lead.

(They begin to slow dance.)

SHEILA: I've been waiting for you forever.

JACK: Huh?

SHEILA: I got the booze.

JACK: What booze?

SHEILA: Two four-packs of Bartles and Jaymes and a bottle of Jose. Do you think that's enough? Maybe I should have gotten some beer. Did you make the reservations?

JACK: Reservations?

SHEILA: For the room.

JACK: Room?

SHEILA: Tahoe. The lake. Where we're going tonight.

JACK: Tonight?

SHEILA: Stop fooling around.

JACK: Sheila —

SHEILA: If you didn't get us a room, I will kill you. Slowly, with great attention to pain.

JACK: Wait. Don't freak out. I think I remember now. We're going to Lake Tahoe, right? Yeah. Tahoe! We're finally gonna do it!

SHEILA: If you're a good boy.

JACK: Oh my God! The trip to Tahoe! I'm going to ask you to marry me!

SHEILA: *(Pause.)* You are?

JACK: Don't you remember?

SHEILA: Remember what?

JACK: *(He stops dancing.)* Sheila, what day is it?

SHEILA: Thursday.

JACK: No. I mean . . . how old are you?

SHEILA: Are you trying to piss me off?

JACK: No.

SHEILA: Remember how we had the party last night? The cake and presents and the card and all that! The Jagermeister? You threw up on

Vince, and I had to drive you home. You puked all over the side of my car. Any of this ringing a bell?

JACK: Your birthday party at the beach.

SHEILA: My twenty-first birthday party, which officially begins tomorrow, which is what you are taking me to Tahoe for. You are such a moron sometimes. So, did you make the reservations or not?

JACK: Yeah. I did make a reservation. For two. Mr. and Mrs. Yeats.

SHEILA: I swear to God, you're such a freak. What is it about you and William Butler Yeats?

JACK: I don't know. I just liked him, I guess.

SHEILA: I did like the one you put in my card.

JACK: Card?

SHEILA: "Tread softly because you tread on my dreams." That's nice. I think I'm gonna paint that. In fact, I've just decided, I am definitely going to paint that poem, the essence of it. The title: "Dream Treading."

JACK: "He wishes for the cloths of Heaven!" *(Quoting from memory, as if he has said this many times before.)*

"Had I the heaven's embroidered cloths,
Enwrought with golden and silver light,
The blue and the dim and the dark cloths
Of night and light and the half-light,
I would spread the cloths under your feet;
But I, being poor, have only my dreams;
I have spread my dreams under your feet;
Tread softly because you tread on my dreams."

(Amazed that he remembered the whole poem.)

SHEILA: I'm gonna tread all over your ass this weekend.

JACK: I remember that. Didn't I make you a mix tape for the drive?

SHEILA: It's in the car right now. I can't believe you put Journey on it.

JACK: Journey rocks. They always make me think of you.

SHEILA: Journey? Do the Dead Kennedys make you think of me too?

JACK: Sometimes. Hey, it's way past midnight. Happy birthday Sheila.

SHEILA: Jesus. I'm twenty-one. I can't believe it. I remember when twenty-one seemed so old. How can that be? How can I possibly be twenty-one? When did that happen? I'm old.

JACK: Yeah.

SHEILA: This is the last birthday where I get something worthwhile. Legal drinking. What do you get that's worth a turd after that?

JACK: I don't know.

SHEILA: I should make a painting about this. The title: "The Last Turd-worthy Birthday."

JACK: Sheila, what are you doing here?

SHEILA: We're going to Tahoe.

JACK: But you're . . . you know . . . why are you here?

SHEILA: This is where you said to meet. We'll have my first legal drink, and then it's off to Tahoe.

JACK: Yeah, but . . . we went to Tahoe . . . a long time ago. Didn't we?

SHEILA: What are you talking about?

JACK: Yeah. We got in a big wreck. Don't you remember?

SHEILA: *(She stares at Jack for a moment, beginning to remember, then violently shakes it off.)* I don't want to talk about that! It's July 3, 1988, and we are going to Tahoe. *(Goes to door, opens it.)* We are getting a room at Circus Circus under the name of Mr. and Mrs. William Butler Yeats, we are going to win at twenty-one and lose at craps, we are going to have sex for the first time, and the second, you are going to get drunk and ask me to marry you. I am going to get even drunker and say yes, or actually "groovy," but I mean yes, and then . . . and then . . . we . . . *(She looks out the door for a moment, then lets it shut.)*

JACK: And then we decided to take a drive around the lake.

SHEILA: You just had to show me Casiopeia and Scorpio and all that astronomy crap you learned in Boy Scouts.

JACK: Webelos.

SHEILA: Whatever. So we go driving around the lake. And we stop halfway around and go swimming. And the water is freezing. So we get out. And you hear a wolf howl.

JACK: I remember. *(Howls.)* And we warm each other up in the back of the car.

SHEILA: Yeah. Third time's the charm. And then we finish the Cuervo.

JACK: And you wanted to stay there. Sleep in the car. But I wanted to stay in the hotel.

SHEILA: Ah, fuck.

JACK: I don't remember what happened after that.

SHEILA: I remember. I woke up after the crash. I couldn't feel anything. The stars were really bright. I could make out Scorpio just above the trees, right where you said he'd be. I thought it would make a great painting. The title: "Star/Scorpion/Blood in the High Sierra." I could see you in the car, your head against the smashed windshield. Fucking seatbelts. One little click, and I could have still been in the car with you. Isn't that funny? One little click. God, I wish I had my paints! Then I just . . . went elsewhere. And now . . . now I guess I'm supposed to be wrapped up in the cloths of Heaven, Jack. But I don't want that. I want to stay here with you. You gave me your dreams, and I'm keeping them.

JACK: My dreams?

SHEILA: There are worse places to hang out. *(Looks out the door, hearing something in the distance.)* I gotta go now.

JACK: Not yet!

SHEILA: "Were you but lying cold and dead,
    And lights were paling out of the West,
    You would come hither, and bend your head,
    And I would lay my head on your breast."
    (Starts to leave.)

JACK: Wait. I don't remember that one!

SHEILA: Bye, Jack.

JACK: Sheila, wait!
    (She stops.)

JACK: I wanted to tell you something. You . . . you look really nice tonight. *(She smiles, and leaves.)*

JACK: Hey, was that last one Yeats too? *(He waits for a reply for a moment. The music from the jukebox changes.)* Who did that? Sheila? You there?

LIMONADE TOUS LES JOURS
Charles L. Mee

Jacqueline is an attractive French woman in her twenties. Andrew is a middle-aged American man. They have been having a love affair. They are having a lemonade in a café.

They are in a café amidst the hundred trees. They are having dessert.

ANDREW: You'll have a limonade?

JACQUELINE: Yes, bien sur.

(He looks around for a waiter.)

You see.

We've had a good time together.

This has been a nice little romance after all.

ANDREW: Yes. Yes, it certainly has.

JACQUELINE: We were afraid to have a fling.

I won't speak for you.

I was afraid

but it turns out it was OK.

ANDREW: Yes.

JACQUELINE: And I hope, when you go back home, you will keep me in a good place in your heart.

ANDREW: Yes. I will.

I certainly will.

JACQUELINE: You know, in France,

this is how it is

you have a lovely time

you hold your life with a light touch

and it's not a tragedy.

ANDREW: Right.

JACQUELINE: All we did was talk about how we can't get together and all the time we got together anyway.

ANDREW: Right.

JACQUELINE: Because we liked it.

ANDREW: Yes.

JACQUELINE: We thought
 we are too damaged
 we can't do this
 because of our histories
 they hold us in a grip and
 we can't go on
 but then we do.

ANDREW: Yes.

JACQUELINE: We don't go on to be together, of course,
 because still
 when we are just being quiet and considerate with each other
 still we know
 it's not right for us
 because we are grown-ups.

ANDREW: Right.

JACQUELINE: Because we are different in age.

ANDREW: Yes.

JACQUELINE: And because we still do have our histories
 they don't go away all at once
 a person cannot suddenly
 all over again become a different person.

ANDREW: Yes.

JACQUELINE: And because you are still a little boring.

ANDREW: I know.

JACQUELINE: And you have some ways of being I don't know
 I won't say I don't have some ways of being that aren't wrong
 but with me
 these ways of being are passing things
 because I am young
 and maybe I don't know any better
 or anyway I will learn
 because I will see what these bad ways of being get me into

and I won't like it

and I will have other ways of being.

ANDREW: Yes.

JACQUELINE: But you.

I don't mean to say:

after all, you are a nice person, I think

ANDREW: Thank you.

JACQUELINE: and I think you still have the capacity to learn

ANDREW: I hope so!

JACQUELINE: and nothing is to be said against a person

who is so considerate

a real gentleman I think

ANDREW: Thank you.

JACQUELINE: but still

with you, you have some ways of being that you have

because they are so old

and you haven't gotten over them

and even if I wouldn't care

because I would love you

you know

I would see right through your ways of being to you yourself

and say, well, so what

he's a little stupid

but he's a nice guy underneath it all

even so, after I would do all that

still the things I think are fun

you think are silly

and what you find interesting

to me is just incredibly tedious.

ANDREW: That could be.

JACQUELINE: So finally you would bore me to tears

I wouldn't be able to stand it

I would be feeling guilty about it

because here you would still be

being considerate and supportive and generous and loving

and I would just want to hit you in the face with a frying pan
so it would be wrong
it would be bad
that would be no fun for you.

ANDREW: No.

JACQUELINE: So, if we have had our little fling
and you go back to America
and I go back to my life
maybe we think of each other

ANDREW: Yes.

JACQUELINE: and we think of each other in a way of warmth and affection

ANDREW: Yes. I know I will.

JACQUELINE: and I think
OK maybe a man is not such a bad thing
and I could have a life with another man

ANDREW: Right.

JACQUELINE: and you could think maybe a woman is not such an evil species
and you will find someone
or you will have your old friend
because an old friend is a good thing
and when you get to be your age
probably this is more important than anything else.

ANDREW: A friend?

JACQUELINE: Yes. And solace
and, you know, getting ready to calm down
to enjoy being in the twilight of your life
wallowing in that a little bit so you don't miss it
and you don't have some frantic bimbo
trying all the time to get you out of the house.

ANDREW: Right.

JACQUELINE: You can have your grandchildren.
And they will play around your feet
next to the dog

and you will doze off in the afternoon sunlight coming through the
window

I think this will be good for you.

ANDREW: You do.

JACQUELINE: And me, I am at the beginning

I want some excitement, you know,

I am going to want to travel quite a lot

and maybe even have sex with a lot of guys

who knows?

Or maybe not

because I am not so wild

or just looking for the thrills

but to be free to be with whoever it is I want

to have the adventures

it's a little bit, you know,

with each person

you enter into their world

you live in their world for a while

it is like a trip to the moon

ANDREW: Yes.

JACQUELINE: to step into their lives for a while

it is to have another entire life for yourself

ANDREW: Yes, it certainly is.

JACQUELINE: and a person wants these things

to have many lives in one life

not a thousand lives maybe

because then you don't notice any one of them

but to have some lives

since you won't have another chance if you only have one life yourself.

ANDREW: Yes.

JACQUELINE: Or you might say

why can't you find all people in one person?

ANDREW: Right.

JACQUELINE: This is what a man I once knew used to say

I was interested in him

in a romantic way
and I tried to seduce him
I have to admit it
and he was in love with another woman
and I said to him
how can you just be faithful to her
isn't this a little boring
because if you would be with me, too,
then it's another whole world for you to live in before you die

ANDREW: Yes.

JACQUELINE: and he said
yes, but,
with this woman I love
I find all the women of the world in one woman
and I thought
oh, yes, well, this could be what people want
and they never find it.

ANDREW: Right.

JACQUELINE: So
you are leaving.
You wish I would drop you at Pascal's?

ANDREW: I can find my own way.
Thanks.

JACQUELINE: I'll say good-bye then.
Probably I won't ever see you again.
Probably not
not for a million years.

ANDREW: Right.
Well.
Good-bye then.
(Do they shake hands or kiss good-bye?
The lights sweep at once to darkness.
Music: the first few bars of a intro to a song.
A spotlight.
Dim, smoky light.
A microphone.

Jacqueline steps up to the microphone and sings.
A French cabaret love song
A French cabaret love song
A French cabaret love song
A French cabaret love song
A French cabaret love song
A French cabaret love song
A French cabaret love song
A French cabaret love song
A French cabaret love song
A French cabaret love song
A French cabaret love song
A French cabaret love song
A French cabaret love song
A French cabaret love song
A French cabaret love song
A French cabaret love song
At the end of her song,
she turns, and Andrew is standing there
with his hand out to her.
She takes his hand.)
JACQUELINE: Oh.
(Silence.)
ANDREW: How time flies.
(Silence.)
JACQUELINE: Yes.
(He leads her back into the darkness as the lights fade to black.)

MONTHS ON END
Craig Pospisil

Elaine and Walter are both thirty-somethings who meet at a New Year's Eve party. Elaine is jealous of all her female friends, all of whom seem to have no trouble finding a steady beau. She's about ready to give up on love until she meets Walter, whose only flaw appears to be that he is married. In this scene, they meet for the first time.

> *The lights come up on Elaine, a depressed-looking woman in her early thirties. She wears an evening dress and nurses a glass of champagne. She has already had several. She surveys the party with distaste. Walter, also in his thirties, enters. He wears a tuxedo. He notices Elaine by herself and crosses to her.*

WALTER: Well . . . a new year.

ELAINE: Yeah.

WALTER: So far it feels pretty much like last year.

ELAINE: Which sucked.

WALTER: Well, it's less than a minute old. Give it time.

ELAINE: To really, really suck.

WALTER: *(Pause.)* Last year was bad for you then?

ELAINE: The. Worst.

WALTER: Why? Or shouldn't I ask?

ELAINE: Well, let's see . . . it began with my dog dying of kidney failure.

WALTER: Oh, I'm sorry. That's a hard thing.

ELAINE: I'd just moved. Been in my new place for about a week when all of a sudden she stops eating. Stops moving really.

WALTER: How old was she?

ELAINE: Fifteen.

WALTER: That's pretty old for a dog, isn't it?

ELAINE: Oh, she was old so she deserved to die?

WALTER: No, course not. I just mean they don't live much longer than that normally. I'm sure she had a good life.

ELAINE: I guess. I just miss her little face when I come home at night. She always perked me up.

WALTER: That's the nice thing about a pet. That unconditional love.

ELAINE: There certainly wasn't any other face to greet me when I got home.

WALTER: Ah, yes. Being alone can be hard . . . but I think solitude is under-rated. It's important to have time by yourself. To just . . . be. *(Slight pause.)* Relationships can be harder than being alone sometimes.

ELAINE: Tell me about it. I've spent plenty of time in relationship hell.

WALTER: That's not quite what I meant, but . . . well, it's hard to find the right person.

ELAINE: No, I find all too many of them. I've had nine boyfriends in the last year.

WALTER: And they say all the good men are married or gay.

ELAINE: Although, calling them boyfriends is a stretch. The only reason I can do it is because I changed my definition. *(Slight pause.)* I mean, just when does a guy change from a date into a boyfriend? Is it walks in the park? Holding hands at the movies? Who knows. *(Slight pause.)* So, I decided that a guy became a boyfriend after four dates or the first time he stays for breakfast. Whichever comes first. *(Slight pause.)* And bang . . . within a couple of months I was able to say I'd had three boyfriends.

WALTER: Congratulations, I guess.

ELAINE: Yeah, now I don't feel like I'm alone, just a loser. *(Slight pause.)* They all dumped me, of course. A little after the fifth date I started hearing, "I'm not ready for a big commitment," or "I need to find who I am first," or "I've got to get home to my wife."

WALTER: At least they came out and said, "That's it." Not everyone does that. Some people go for years wanting to get out of a relationship, but they're too scared to say anything. Or they don't know how. *(Slight pause.)* Consider yourself lucky.

ELAINE: You're driving me nuts, you know that.

WALTER: Am I? I'm sorry.

ELAINE: Stop trying to put a positive spin on everything. It's New Year's

Eve. People are supposed to be depressed. *(Slight pause.)* The whole holiday is made up anyway.

WALTER: Aren't they all?

ELAINE: Oh, shut up.

WALTER: Look, things could always be worse. Don't go around adding up everything that's wrong with your life. You've got to focus on what's right.

ELAINE: Is that supposed to make me feel better?

WALTER: A little, yes.

ELAINE: Well, it doesn't! *(Slight pause.)* I hate that philosophy. Sure, things could be worse. I could have cancer. There could be a nuclear war. The Earth could decide to stop spinning on its axis. *(Slight pause.)* So what?! Does that make me any less lonely? Will I sleep better tonight? *(She puts the glass down and digs in her purse for a Kleenex. She blows her nose loudly and starts to cry.)* Christ, how did I wind up here? Every damn New Year's I find myself at some stranger's apartment. And they're always living better lives than me. Look at this place. It's enormous.

WALTER: Oh, don't fall into that trap. Just because someone has money doesn't mean they're happy.

ELAINE: You really have to stop that. *(Slight pause.)* What makes it worse, too, is these people have no taste. Did you see that painting in the other room? What is that? It looks like a leprechaun on acid.

WALTER: So, what brought you here?

ELAINE: *What* indeed. *(Slight pause.)* I'm on a date. A really, really lousy date.

WALTER: Oh? Where is he?

ELAINE: See that guy over there by the kitchen door? The one with the curly, dark hair? The one with the broad shoulders and great cheekbones!

WALTER: The one kissing my wife?

ELAINE: Yeah. *(She does a double take.)* What?

WALTER: You weren't the only one having a bad year.

ELAINE: But you. . . . how can . . . ? Oh, God, I'm sorry.

WALTER: Why? You're not kissing her.

ELAINE: Yeah, but here I am going on and on about . . . I mean, this is only our third date and no breakfast. That's your wife.

WALTER: It seems like I've been waiting for this moment for months. The element of surprise is gone.

ELAINE: Still, I mean . . . hey . . . where'd they go?

WALTER: Down the hall to the bedroom.

ELAINE: How can you just stand there? Why don't you leave?

WALTER: I live here. With the leprechaun.

ELAINE: My, this year is off to a good start. *(Pause.)* I'm sorry.

WALTER: No, forget it. I hate it too. Nina did most of the decorating. The only thing I like are the Africa masks.

ELAINE: Oh, yes, yes. Those are lovely. *(Pause.)* I think maybe I'll go. Except my coat's in the bedroom.

WALTER: Would you like a glass of champagne?

ELAINE: I think I've had enough.

WALTER: Are you sure? It's very good champagne.

ELAINE: Yes, I know. It's quickly replacing all the blood in my brain.

WALTER: Well, if you won't drink any, would you at least help me pour it down the drain?

ELAINE: Pour Dom Perignon down the drain? Why?

WALTER: It occurs to me that if the champagne was gone maybe all these people would decide to leave. And head to the bedroom for their coats.

ELAINE: *(Slight pause.)* Why, yes, I could use another glass.

WALTER: Right this way. *(Slight pause.)* Oh, wait . . . what's your name?

ELAINE: Elaine.

WALTER: I'm Walter.

ELAINE: Nice to meet you.

WALTER: You too. Here's to a New Year. *(Walter offers Elaine his arm and they exit. Fade to black.)*

THE NINTH CIRCLE
Edward Musto

Tom and Alley are both in their thirties. They have just had sex in a fleabag hotel room. This is the opening scene of the play.

> *A small dark room at the American Hotel on East 86th Street, New York City. It is 5:30 in the afternoon. The date is Tuesday, November 4, 1980. The only light peeps in from between the slats of a broken set of blinds. Sitting by the window is Tom. Thirty-five years of age. Winsome, boy-next-door looks, though age has begun its descent. He is peering through the blinds. Naked, he turns to take in the bed. Alley is facing him, her nakedness hidden by dingy sheets she has drawn up over her. Tom holds up his pack of cigarettes. She nods. He tosses her the pack. It falls onto the bed. She jams cigarettes up, takes one out, then reaches for a small box of wooden matches. She lights her cigarette.*

ALLEY: Stay.
TOM: I can't.
ALLEY: Just for fun.
TOM: Wish I could.
ALLEY: Not asking for marriage.
TOM: Good thing. I already am.
ALLEY: Wanna go out?
TOM: Some other time.
ALLEY: Yeah, you're right. What's the point?
TOM: Well, don't be *hurt,* for Chrissake.
ALLEY: Fuck you.
   (Pause.)
TOM: Saw a rat in the street today.
ALLEY: A live one?
TOM: Got run over by a car or something. This glop of gray mesh with

a splash of red in the middle. It was on the corner of Eightieth and Fifth.

ALLEY: Probably it was a pigeon that got run over.

TOM: No, it was a rat. There was a tail.

ALLEY: You should have brought it. We could have made soup.

TOM: Like they really allow cooking in the rooms.

ALLEY: I'm famished.

TOM: So am I.

ALLEY: Maybe we could go for a bite.

TOM: Got too much on my plate already.

ALLEY: It's just as well.

TOM: Sorry, though.

ALLEY: I *said* it's just as well.

TOM: What time do you have?

ALLEY: Five-thirty.

TOM: I'm sitting here like I have the whole afternoon to piss away.

ALLEY: You already have. It's practically night.

TOM: For your information it isn't practically night.

ALLEY: Evening officially begins at six o'clock.

TOM: Who says?

ALLEY: *TV Guide.*

    (Pause.)

TOM: Didn't even get to vote.

ALLEY: Is *that* what you were doing at the school?

TOM: What else?

ALLEY: Thought you might be on the make for one of the kids.

TOM: You did not think that.

    (Pause.)

ALLEY: Do you bite your nails?

TOM: Why do you want to know?

ALLEY: Just wondering.

TOM: Kind of personal, that.

ALLEY: Skip it then.

    (Pause.)

TOM: No. I don't bite them.

ALLEY: Usually I can tell without having to ask.

TOM: Bite *your* nails, do you?

ALLEY: For years I did. Scraped the enamel right off the corner of one of my front teeth and it came off. You can barely notice it, even if you're up close. A shrink would say I'm eating myself up with something. Try as I may I can't seem to stop. What I used to do with my *nails* I now do with the *cuticles.* Why my fingertips are in such appalling condition. I'd stop if I could. Keep meaning to. But before I realize it my fingers are in my mouth and I'm ripping off big chunks of skin from around the nails. The more I do it, the more I have to. No matter how much it hurts, no matter how much blood I draw. Know what I do sometimes? If it's a large piece of skin I stick it on the end of a match and watch it burn.

TOM: Do you teach first or second grade?

ALLEY: First. Ever watch flesh burning? *(She bites at her nails.)* Look closely now. This patch of skin. It'll catch fire, turn black around the edges, then liquefy, bubble, and bloom into ash. *(She blows out the match.)* Wanna go eat?

TOM: Told you. I can't.

ALLEY: Yeah, you're right. I've got things to do, anyway. Grade papers. Plan lessons.

TOM: Mold America's future.

ALLEY: Only got into teaching for all the time off. Out at three every day. Summers off. Spring breaks, too. All the holidays. Leaves me plenty of time for myself.

TOM: And for hotel rooms where they rent by the hour. Creepy smell.

ALLEY: Small price to pay. Cleansing effect of fire and all that. Who did you vote for today?

TOM: No one. There wasn't time. I met you, fell in love. We came directly here.

ALLEY: Who are you going to vote for?

TOM: Don't think I'll be able to. Have to get home.

ALLEY: Who *would* you have voted for then?

TOM: At the office everyone's voting for Reagan.

ALLEY: What do you do?

TOM: I'm a recovering parochial school boy.

ALLEY: Fuck. Don't tell me.

TOM: Corporate outplacement.

ALLEY: What's that?

TOM: The company I work for does corporate outplacement.

ALLEY: But what *is* that?

TOM: Counseling for the unemployed.

ALLEY: How do you make money from *that?*

TOM: Businesses pay us.

ALLEY: So you're like an employment agency?

TOM: The companies that have hired us are the same companies that have fired the people we're counseling.

ALLEY: And what do they get for their money? I assume it costs them plenty. What do they get?

TOM: Peace of mind. *(He lights a cigarette.)* I must've been really hot for you. Got buttons missing. You see, these days it's in the best interests of a company to do everything it can for an exec before showing him the door. Cuts down on hard feelings, cuts down on lawsuits. The process isn't even referred to as anything but outplacement. Nobody's let go anymore. Nobody's fired, sacked, terminated, or otherwise given the push. Everybody's outplaced. Everybody's happy.

ALLEY: How many companies are there like yours?

TOM: Right now only a handful. And at the top of that short list is Hite, Upton & Curtis, which since 1974 has provided the finest in corporate outplacement. All individual programs feature career counseling, mock interviews on the Betamax with professional feedback, résumé preparation, mailings, blah, blah, blah.

ALLEY: Spoken like a glossy brochure.

TOM: We also offer group outplacement, retirement planning, spouse counseling, and seminars on stress management.

ALLEY: Blah, blah, and more blah.

TOM: My watch must be slow. What time have you got?

ALLEY: Seven minutes later than the last time you asked.

TOM: I've got to get home.

　　　(Pause.)

ALLEY: Want my phone number?

TOM: Sure.

ALLEY: Yeah, you're right. What's the point?

TOM: Nothing personal.

ALLEY: I know.

TOM: Just that I rarely go back for seconds.

ALLEY: Same here.

TOM: It was nice, though.

ALLEY: For me, too.

TOM: Maybe we'll run into each other again sometime.

ALLEY: Stranger things have happened.

TOM: Gotta make a pit stop. Get dressed if you want to leave together.
    (They dress.)

TOM: Fuck.

ALLEY: What's the matter?

TOM: Damn place is infested.

ALLEY: Better shake out our clothing before we leave.

TOM: Except it ain't roaches.

ALLEY: Place has mice. What a surprise.

TOM: Larger than that.

ALLEY: Well, I doubt you saw a *rat.* They only come out at night. It's only
    quarter to six.

TOM: Maybe they don't get *TV Guide.*

ALLEY: Rats never come out during the day. They're photophobic. Afraid
    of the light.

TOM: Give me a cigarette.

ALLEY: What's the magic word?

TOM: Give-me-a-cigarette-or-I'll-kick-your-rotten-head-in.

ALLEY: You're more fun *out* of your clothes than *in* 'em.

TOM: Through yet?

ALLEY: Where's my other shoe?

TOM: I don't see it anywhere.

ALLEY: You aren't even looking.

TOM: Because it's not my shoe.

ALLEY: Such a fuck-head thou art. C'mon. I can't leave without it.

TOM: It's got to *be* here.

ALLEY: Check under the bed.

TOM: Why can't you?

ALLEY: Nice to know chivalry isn't dead.

TOM: Chivalry is *not* what you wanted from me.

ALLEY: Found it.

TOM: Almost ready?

ALLEY: Zip me up.

TOM: *(Slight disdain.)* Anyone'd think we're married.

ALLEY: Perish the thought.

(Pause.)

TOM: Something I said?

ALLEY: Ignore me. Always in a bad mood after I get laid.

TOM: Yeah. Me, too.

ALLEY: *(Taking out a cigarette.)* One for the road?

TOM: Make it quick.

(Tom, in front of a mirror, fastens his tie. Alley stares thoughtfully at him for a moment.)

ALLEY: You're actually somebody's husband.

TOM: Hey, we all make mistakes.

ALLEY: Live in town?

TOM: Eighty-fifth and Second.

ALLEY: Children?

TOM: Bite your tongue.

ALLEY: Tell me about your wife.

TOM: Her name is Catherine. She is the perfect woman. Beauty, brains, the works. She manages a marketing research firm, is an accomplished musician, and a gourmet cook. She's good with money, good with people, good with everything.

ALLEY: Who's *she* voting for?

TOM: Often wish I didn't resent her quite as much as I do.

ALLEY: Enjoying the view?

TOM: Mm-hmm.

ALLEY: No false modesty in you, is there?

TOM: Absolutely none, either false or genuine.

ALLEY: Well, you get points for honesty, anyway.

TOM: Something my first grade teacher used to say. No matter how badly you fucked up, she went easier on you if you 'fessed up to it.

ALLEY: *(Squinting her eyes.)* Trying to picture you as a little kid. Having a rough time of it.

TOM: Imagine someone awkward and shy and nothing much to look at. My teacher worried my self-imposed isolation wasn't healthy and determined the best way for me to get over my inadequacies was to force me into a situation that was pregnant with social intercourse. She cast me in the school play. My teacher was way ahead of her time. Must have thought she was going to set progressive education ablaze with this gender-fuck version of *Sleeping Beauty.* In it the Prince of Coldness, a mythical place where it's always winter, angers the evil warlock, who turns him into ice. Only a kiss can save him. He's about to be done in by said evil warlock when in the nick of time he's rescued by a nearby lumber*jill.* She kisses him on the mouth. He melts before her eyes.

ALLEY: And you were the evil warlock?

TOM: I was the ice prince.

ALLEY: Oh.

TOM: Finish up now.

ALLEY: Sure; no problem. Certainly there's no reason why I should hang around *this* dump. I've got my *own* dump to hang around in. Not to mention the usual haunts.

TOM: Plato's Retreat, the Inferno, etc.

ALLEY: You know the Inferno?

TOM: Sure do.

ALLEY: There a lot?

TOM: Once in a while.

ALLEY: Surprised we've never run into each other.

TOM: Who's to say we haven't?

ALLEY: *(Small laugh.)* It *is* pretty dimly lit.

TOM: Adds to the ambiance.

ALLEY: Maybe next time you go I'll be there.

TOM: Never can tell. Got your coat?

ALLEY: I'm all set.

TOM: Shall we, then?

(He moves to kiss her.)

ALLEY: Hey! What are you doing?

TOM: I'm sorry. I was going to kiss you. I forgot I don't know you.

ALLEY: All right. I guess you weren't trying to be familiar.

TOM: Really. I wasn't.

ALLEY: Maybe we shouldn't leave together.

TOM: No, it's okay. C'mon. I'll drop you.

ALLEY: You're taking a cab? I thought you were going home. And isn't that
practically around the corner from here?

TOM: Just remembered I told my secretary to meet me.

ALLEY: Where?

TOM: Seventy-third and Lex.

ALLEY: And you're gonna take a *cab?*

TOM: You want a lift or not?

ALLEY: How far can you bring me? My place is way downtown.

TOM: Ten blocks. Take it or leave it.

ALLEY: Never mind.

TOM: Just that I'm already late.

ALLEY: So you said.

TOM: I'd bring you further if it weren't for that.

ALLEY: Maybe I can take the taxi the rest of the way.

TOM: Fine. Let's go now.

ALLEY: Nope. I can't spare the cash. Looks like I'm taking the bus.

TOM: Well, it's been *nice.*

    (Pause.)

ALLEY: Yes.

TOM: I mean it.

ALLEY: So do I.

TOM: Really wish I didn't have to go.

ALLEY: Them's the breaks.

TOM: Guess we should say good-bye here.

ALLEY: Please. Not downstairs.

TOM: I know.

ALLEY: Too something . . . I don't know . . . creepy.

TOM: Good-bye, then.

ALLEY: See you around.

TOM: What's your name?

ALLEY: Alley.

TOM: Alley.

ALLEY: Yours?

TOM: Tom.

ALLEY: We'll see each other again.

TOM: Think so?

ALLEY: We're bound to.

　　(Blackout.)

OTHER PEOPLE
Christopher Shinn

This scene takes place in a strip club. Petra, an aspiring poet who is also a stripper, in her twenties, is having an intellectual conversation with a customer, who could be any age.

PETRA: Before he died, then, you actually knew him.

MAN: I used to go to this diner all the time he worked at, you know, by where I work, the show was going up, we were all real excited for him — he was just our waiter, at the time.

PETRA: Wow.

MAN: Do you like it? You've seen it?

PETRA: I have.

MAN: You said you lived in the East Village, so I —

PETRA: No, I understand.

MAN: I mean, you're not — perhaps I'm being dumb, or presumptuous. I mean, what do I know? . . .

PETRA: You're not being dumb.

MAN: But you don't like the show, or? The critics, they liked it, people, young people seem to — standing ovation the night I saw it — Pulitzer Prize. So I'm interested in why, if — isn't that — East Village — but — why don't you talk.

PETRA: Look — thirteen-year-old kids, fat girls, gay boys, they love it, so. I don't, truly, I don't think about it. No. If I did think about it I would get angry because. Because it's another example of. It's — *condescending.*

MAN: How is that?

PETRA: Because. Because I work hard and. I work to try and be an *artist* — which, it's an embarrassment to even use that word —

MAN: Why?

PETRA: Listen — I read. I work hard. And what the show says to me is — is am I indecent, or, or am "selling out" or am I *inauthentic* because

I want, I want money or, or an apartment which is even just *decent?* I mean when do any of those characters *read?* What are they *doing* with all their time, I don't — and we *celebrate* these people, and don't get me wrong, everyone is *valuable*, but, but *what* are we celebrating?

MAN: Life. The artistic life. Refusal to compromise. Right?

PETRA: Wanna know who lives in the East Village? A lot of the actors in the show that's who. Those characters, it's like Peter Pan Neverland, refusing to grow up, join the real — I know it's a *musical* but it avoids asking any real, I mean, *genuine* questions and instead makes — makes a mockery of my roommate said this and I agree — makes a *spectacle* of AIDS, gays, lesbians, blacks — it — *commodifies* actual — and tell me these people who are in it and who directed it have no idea how they're mocking themselves and their — their own *choices* — oh whatever.

MAN: No, no, please, this is! — You're . . . how can I say this . . . threatened by them. By these characters.

PETRA: Well. What I was going to say was. I'm not used to having to think too hard when I'm here.

MAN: Change the subject then. I want to hear one of your poems.

PETRA: Oh come on.

MAN: Why are you embarrassed? My goodness, the fact that you write poems — is fascinating to me! Would you tell me one?

PETRA: I, they're written down, so.

MAN: See, you are just — who you are — comes through and is — fascinating! So. So I know this isn't — I'm not stupid — *(He takes out his wallet.)* I'm under no — *(He puts money on the table.)* There. For a poem. For one poem.

PETRA: I'll talk to you but. No.

MAN: Okay. Okay. We talk. Here: I just saw this movie? *Boogie Nights?* What did you think of it?

PETRA: All those movies, *Trainspotting, Boogie Nights,* I — I can't.

MAN: Can't? . . . You don't . . . obviously don't.

PETRA: It's immoral because . . . I live in *this world* and — they — romanticize — and *ignore* — they leave out of this *experience,* this, being *alive* — and I think: Is this what I must include? To be *valued?*

Rewarded? *Depravity?* To be seen must I write what is more or less — more or less *pornography*, something that *titillates* with violence and sex? Or else — *My Best Friend's Wedding* and *The Celestine Prophecy?* Do you see?

MAN: I come here you know.

PETRA: You . . . ?

MAN: You say: I live in this world. And I am interested in your opinions. I ask you about these plays and movies, which *I* see, which *you* see . . .

PETRA: I don't understand what you meant by "I come here." You come here?

MAN: Here. How can I . . .?

PETRA: Oh — it just gets me so angry. Drugs — drugs are not — violence, real violence, life, *life* — the poor, criminals, it is not — we romanticize it — it is like — a drug — like — the trauma, the trauma of actually seeing this world is such that we create fantasies, we reward those who create *fantasies* because God forbid we look at — reality — at *ourselves* — there are people in this country, *other people* who are fascinating and, and *troubled* — and yet — where are they? — and New York and Los Angeles constantly dump this — shit this shit into this country, and people will — eat it because they're *hungry* — these *crumbs* — and I don't — I'm not judging those who watch or, or *read* this stuff — I watch it too sometimes — but I blame those who — look — I am trying to *transcend* — but there are pressures which prevent me — many *pressures* and — I mean you say: You say, I come here. I say: I work here.

MAN: I come here for fantasy. Is what I was going to say. And what is so wrong with fantasy? If that's what we need to live. Because. Don't we all have fantasies?

PETRA: But there's a moral . . . in terms of *art* . . . *(She stops.)* I'm sorry.

MAN: Here's the deal. I want you to show me your life. Because it is so distant from my life. This is why I go to movies, and plays. And come here. And so I know, I am aware that perhaps you will find this — distasteful. Or immoral even. But you would get to see my life. Which you, you could not fathom. Where I work. The conversations I have. I am asking for — some time — dinner, dates, you will take me to coffee where you have coffee. I will take you to dinner where I have dinner. I don't — I'm a gentle man — and I am a — frightened man — and curious — and I don't — I know without money I am nothing to you. I am a very rich person, and I have herpes so I don't really have sex anymore. *(Pause.)*

PETRA: Let me ask you this. Why if you are interested in getting to know somebody, in intimacy, why would you come here? To a pornographic place?

MAN: You're right, But I'll pay you not to come here. To accompany me as though —

PETRA: But why — in the first place — you're — you have money — you're nice — and attractive —

MAN: Oh, come now. You tell me, how else might I have met you. In a club? Come up to you in some club in Tribeca, "Hey, how are you?"

PETRA: But — I'm not talking about just *me* —

MAN: I am. I find you fascinating. I don't find my secretary fascinating. I'm sorry. *(Pause.)*

PETRA: I work here, this is my job, I don't go home as this person, I —

MAN: Here. *(He takes out a hundred dollar bill and writes on it.)* Now you can call me and. Call me and just. Talk to me about your life. And then. We can get together and have dinner and coffee a couple of times and I will pay you for your time. *(Rising.)* Take care, Petra. *(He goes. She takes the hundred dollars.)*

THE PARKER FAMILY CIRCUS
Jan Buttram

This comedy takes place in the living room of a small house in Plano, Texas. Tommy, a teenaged boy, is mentally retarded. He spends most of his time hanging out at his grandmother's house. Vesta, also a teenager, is a friend of Tommy's sister. She has something of an entrepreneurial mentality and sees in Tommy's comic book collection a golden business opportunity.

Vesta eyes the stack of funny books.

VESTA: You told Virgil Rivera you're selling your comic books.

TOMMY: I need some money. I'm moving in here with Mamaw and I have to get the T.V. fixed.

VESTA: Remember the day we read them together, you and I and your granddad?

TOMMY: So?

VESTA: Your grandfather gave them all to you in writing and all?

TOMMY: I think so.

VESTA: Wow. You possess an extensive and rare collection of comic books.

TOMMY: I know.

VESTA: I liked it where this snake woman saves the world by sucking the venom from the foot of this monster.

TOMMY: Yeah, that was Papaw's favorite. Ramona the revenger. She disguises herself as snakes . . . she covers herself with poisonous snakes so no one will see her. Papaw bought it in 1940.

VESTA: Whoa. Ancient times . . . That's practically stone age comics.

TOMMY: Or before.

VESTA: Which one is your favorite?

TOMMY: I said. Ramona, the revenger.

VESTA: Chill. You said that was your Papaw's.

TOMMY: She's my favorite, too.

VESTA: OK.

TOMMY: She has tits the size of watermelons and they shoot fire. She incinerates the evil forces with her snake tongue.

VESTA: I'd like to read that one. Want to?

TOMMY: No.

VESTA: OK, so . . . How much are you asking for the collection?

TOMMY: I haven't said.

VESTA: Because you haven't decided or you don't know?

TOMMY: Uh, not saying I don't know.

VESTA: Could we read one now?

TOMMY: No.

VESTA: Well, could I look at them?

TOMMY: No! Leave me alone.

VESTA: Would you consider a barter deal?

TOMMY: What is that?

VESTA: Where you give a person something they want for something you want.

TOMMY: I don't want nothing from nobody.

VESTA: I know where you are. I was like that for a long time. I'd just see everything as bad and not care about nothing. But there's good things. *(Beat.)* I'd like to sit in your lap. *(Tommy is quiet. She does.)* You asked that slut Tandy Woo to have sex. Why didn't you ask me?

TOMMY: I don't know.

VESTA: Well, ask me.

TOMMY: I found someone.

VESTA: You did?

TOMMY: Mamaw.

VESTA: Your grandmother?

TOMMY: Yes.

VESTA: What about her?

TOMMY: She's goin' to have sex with me.

VESTA: Isn't she kinda old?

TOMMY: I don't think so.

(Vesta snuggles up to him.)

VESTA: And, you *want* to have sex with her?

TOMMY: I like her.

VESTA: Don't you like me?

TOMMY: Not a whole lot.

VESTA: You let me read your comic books.

TOMMY: You keep callin' them comic books, they're funny books. Papaw called them funny books.

VESTA: OK, funny books.

TOMMY: I let you read one of them the one time, we looked through them with Papaw. I did that.

VESTA: If you and I have sex, then you won't have to bother your grandmother.

(Tommy is silent.)

VESTA: You sign a paper makin' me your sales agent, and I'll sell 'em all and take a percentage off the top . . . say thirty-five percent. I know thirty-five percent is kinda high but as a barter situation . . . I'll also have sex with you.

TOMMY: Hmmnm.

VESTA: It's a good deal. Your mamaw will never have sex with you.

(Tommy pushes Vesta away.)

TOMMY: YES, SHE WILL! GET OFF ME!

(Vesta recovers.)

VESTA: OK, but your mamaw will flip your lights off if you ask her.

TOMMY: I did ask her.

VESTA: And?

TOMMY: She said she would.

VESTA: Wow. Well. Weird. OK, then.

TOMMY: OK.

VESTA: If she changes her mind . . .

TOMMY: About what?

VESTA: If she won't have sex with you . . .

TOMMY: Why would she change her mind?

VESTA: Look, I have a two-year financial growth plan so if your grandmother changes her mind . . . get back to me?

TOMMY: OK. I'm sorry I pushed you.

VESTA: It's OK. And Coach Norris is scared of your mother so he won't press charges.

(A beat.)

TOMMY: If I did give you the funny books to sell for me?

VESTA: Yes?

TOMMY: We could have sex once.

VESTA: Yeah.

TOMMY: But after that I'm going to live with Mamaw.

VESTA: OK. That would be OK.

TOMMY: So don't get crazy if I don't do it more than the one time.

VESTA: No. I could live with it.

RACE
Ferdinand Bruckner, adapted by Barry Edelstein

Karlanner and Helene are both in their twenties and engaged to be married. He is a university student. It's 1933, in Germany, and the Nazis are coming into power. While not a Nazi himself, Karlanner is very intimidated by his fellow students who are, and he has begun to wonder if being engaged to Helene, a Jewish woman, is a bad idea.

Helene's apartment. Helene and Karlanner have finished dinner.

HELENE: *(Relaxed and comfortable.)* So you decided to vote after all.

KARLANNER: Tessow came over at eight this morning. I would've missed the lecture. This endless apartment hunting . . .

HELENE: Was it interesting?

KARLANNER: We all sang together. The professor walked in and . . . I wasn't ready for it. All of sudden, right in the middle of the lecture, he just started singing. I mean, he's sixty! Then at the end, all sorts of new songs, beautiful songs, that I didn't even know.

HELENE: What was he lecturing about that made you sing?

KARLANNER: It was . . . an epiphany. I'll always remember.

HELENE: You should go to lectures more often, even if you're not really learning anything.

KARLANNER: *(Quietly.)* I learned something today, that's for sure.

HELENE: It's bad for you to stay home all the time.

KARLANNER: Then we voted.

HELENE: You have to be around people. It keeps you balanced. Like the office. It does me good, even though all I do is think of you all day.

KARLANNER: *(Hesitates.)* So I voted . . . and then we got something to eat. We spent the whole afternoon outside.

HELENE: Was Sieglemann with you?

KARLANNER: Siegelmann?

HELENE: The three of you were always together.

KARLANNER: When was that?

HELENE: *(Nods.)* You shouldn't neglect your friends like that.

KARLANNER: Tessow dropped me here. He wouldn't leave until I promised to meet him at the Beer Hall at nine. You get the election results faster there. *(Carefully.)* Although I don't really have to go. If the government wins, every bell in the city will ring. We'll hear them right here.

HELENE: Go.

KARLANNER: I should go?

HELENE: I just want to lie down. My legs are sore from all the stairs I climbed. I saw ten apartments today. Maybe one possibility, on Karlstrasse. But the bathroom is too small.

KARLANNER: The bathroom. Don't you want to know how I voted?

HELENE: *(Baby talk.)* How many times in the past year has my big boy voted?

KARLANNER: Your big boy.

HELENE: Another election every month. Five new governments since last summer. It's just a game for big boys.

KARLANNER: This time it might be serious.

HELENE: They're saying that at the office, too. For a while now, every time my boss says hello, it's like he's dropping some kind of hint. Probably because I'm Jewish.

KARLANNER: *(Chokes.)* Probably?

HELENE: *(Laughs.)* Who knows what these middle-management types are thinking.

KARLANNER: *(Malicious.)* You're always so superior.

HELENE: This is the twentieth century. This is Germany.

KARLANNER: I voted for the Jackboot Club. *(Helene looks at him.)* Remember we used to call them the Jackboot Club? *(Waits.)* Actually, it's your name for them.

HELENE: Mine? We read it in the paper a hundred times.

KARLANNER: In the paper *you* get.

HELENE: *(Calmly.)* Yes.

KARLANNER: *(Angered.)* So it isn't yours.

HELENE: I like it, so I use it — All right, it's mine. But you've said it enough.

KARLANNER: Because the master's been eating out of the slave girl's hand.

HELENE: *(Astonished.)* What?

KARLANNER: For years.

HELENE: *(Laughs.)* Is that from some cheap novel or something?

KARLANNER: Laugh.

HELENE: You read that stuff to relax after work? I never knew. *(Warmer.)* You're just full of surprises.

KARLANNER: A big surprise.

HELENE: It's that famous German intellect: true genius on one hand, pulp fiction on the other.

KARLANNER: *(Beside himself.)* Nothing affects you. Nothing.

HELENE: Should it affect me that you voted for the Jackboot Club?

KARLANNER: It's un-German.

HELENE: *(More careful.)* Oh?

KARLANNER: That's all I have to say.

HELENE: *(Pause.)* Do you want to eat?

KARLANNER: No, thank you.

HELENE: *(Gets up, begins to clear the table.)* Tessow voted for the Jackboot Club too?

KARLANNER: The National Socialist German Workers' Party.

HELENE: Force of habit.

KARLANNER: He's been a member for months.

HELENE: That's why you never answered his letters *(Karlanner is silent.)* And I guess that's why you weren't going to class.

KARLANNER: You've got all the answers. I don't even need to talk.

HELENE: *(Quietly.)* Stop it.

KARLANNER: *(Goes to the window.)* Just an anthropological observation.

HELENE: Sometimes I wonder what would have become of me if we'd never met. What is there for a rich man's daughter except a thousand kinds of boredom? I even thought about going on safari. *(Finishes clearing away.)* You saved me from all that. You showed me the beauty of an ordinary life. *(Still simply.)* You made me . . . more real.

KARLANNER: You like a struggle.

HELENE: *(Quietly.)* I'll never run away from one.

KARLANNER: Struggles make life seem more real. But they damage the dream.

HELENE: Which dream?

KARLANNER: Impossible to explain.

HELENE: *(Seriously.)* Maybe what you call the dream is what I call the cheap novel.

KARLANNER: Maybe that's the difference between us. But the soul of the people will take up that cheap novel. We will transform it into an epic poem, into the answer we've been longing for.

HELENE: *(Frightened.)* You've been longing for it too?

KARLANNER: Me too.

HELENE: How long?

KARLANNER: All my life.

HELENE: Why didn't you say anything?

KARLANNER: Because I didn't know until I found it. Because you kept distracting me. Real life, apartments, bathrooms. Meanwhile a storm was breaking over all of Germany.

HELENE: *(More certain.)* I would see you standing outside the office, waiting for me, looking so tired, pale. And my heart would break. I thought you were working overtime to graduate sooner. But now I see. It was really the dream. It wouldn't leave you alone.

KARLANNER: I went to one single meeting, and all your liberal garbage washed off me. — *(Regretful.)* But I never marched in that Stormtrooper Parade. Everybody sang, even the riot police. But I never did.

HELENE: You studied for exams.

KARLANNER: *(Angry.)* What did exams mean at the lecture today? Every heart in that auditorium beat to the same pulse. Every heart but mine. I was alone, apart. But by the second verse, I wasn't alone anymore. I was in the middle of it. Finally . . . I dove in.

HELENE: So now you want to go to the Beer Hall, to dive deeper.

KARLANNER: You don't know anything about it.

HELENE: *(Forcefully.)* When I found you two years ago, you didn't know much either.

KARLANNER: *(Laughs.)* I was a Democrat.

HELENE: You were a drunken bum. You never had an ounce of democracy in you. After a while I gave up trying.

KARLANNER: Lucky for me.

HELENE: But then I got a surprise. The real you, hidden behind the empty face of an alcoholic. We were together all the time. I took care of you. I saved you. I was your nurse.

KARLANNER: You never gave up. One of the qualities of your race.

HELENE: I wanted to, so many times. But I stayed, because I could feel you, behind it all — I can still feel you there, Peter. Even with all you drank today, it's still you.

KARLANNER: *(Gets up.)* I didn't drink anything today.

HELENE: You're talking like you're drunk.

KARLANNER: And you're going to nurse me again.

HELENE: Nurse you.

KARLANNER: I'll keep you in mind.

HELENE: *(Exhausted.)* He'll keep me in mind.

KARLANNER: *(Pause.)* Is that all?

HELENE: Whatever you want.

KARLANNER: *(His watch.)* I have another three minutes. *(Helene stands aside.)* Look, it surprised me, too. *(Sits.)* Just this afternoon I could barely speak to Rosloh without screaming. But during the lecture, the way he stood there . . . singing . . . transported . . . he was like a different man. I never saw him like that.

HELENE: Rosloh?

KARLANNER: *(Nods.)* I understood —

HELENE: Rosloh who started all the craziness at the university?

KARLANNER: I understood that true passion, even if it's completely meaningless, is better than the most rational thinking.

HELENE: You've always hated Rosloh.

KARLANNER: After the lecture I had to talk to him. I couldn't help it. *(Looks away.)* I shook his hand, felt it in mine . . . . the clarity, the certainty that things will make sense again. — I knew I was at the opposite end of the earth from you.

HELENE: The opposite end of the earth from me. Three minutes are up.

KARLANNER: You want me to go?

HELENE: You're already gone. The opposite end of the earth.

KARLANNER: *(Angry.)* We've finished a chapter of our lives. It was a mistake. A beautiful mistake, but still —

HELENE: The mistake was thinking that we were somehow immune from it.

KARLANNER: A mistake. *(Gets up.)*

HELENE: For two years we convinced ourselves. That's a mistake.

KARLANNER: *(Weak.)* But we can see each other once in a while?

HELENE: *(With finality.)* If it hadn't been for the good qualities of my race —

KARLANNER: *(Immediately.)* I never said good.

HELENE: — you'd still be in the same sewer you were two years ago.

KARLANNER: *(Laughs.)* The good.

HELENE: So thank me for them.

KARLANNER: Should I also thank your race?

HELENE: Say thank you and go.

KARLANNER: *(Beside himself.)* To the Jews? You never gave a damn about being a Jew. You were even going to let me decide whether or not you should convert to Christianity.

HELENE: You once told me that a civil ceremony wouldn't be good enough because our marriage was going to be more real.

KARLANNER: I remember that night. You stroked my hair in that way you have and you said, "I could always become a Christian."

HELENE: *(Uneasy.)* Because when you said that it touched me.

KARLANNER: "Anyway, it's just a formality," you said. "We're living in enlightened times."

HELENE: What do you want?

KARLANNER: The formalities were bullshit. You should have stated your position much sooner. It would have made breaking up a lot easier.

HELENE: *(Angry.)* What position?

KARLANNER: That you're a Jew.

HELENE: You call that a position?

KARLANNER: *(Nods.)* I don't speak your language anymore. Get used to it.

HELENE: Did I ever hide the fact that I was Jewish?

KARLANNER: You avoided it. We pretended it wasn't there.

HELENE: So?

KARLANNER: You even said you would deny it if you had to. And I went along with it, like some . . . . accomplice. Then I, as a German —

HELENE: *(Nods.)* You are a German.

KARLANNER: As soon as you state your position clearly, I am just as clearly on the opposite side. We've been too vague. Formalities, enlightened times . . . you've been taking advantage of me. Now the frontlines are clear.

HELENE: *(Looks at him.)* I know nothing about Judaism. You're right.

KARLANNER: The Karlanners have been German for hundreds of years.

There were three generals and all kinds of government officials in my family.

HELENE: My family went to temple once a year. All I remember about it is my father's face. More serious than usual. *(Laughs.)* My only memories of religion . . .

KARLANNER: So. Now that we've stated our positions clearly, our personal affairs are finished.

HELENE: I'm out the door just like that.

KARLANNER: Which is why I consider it my duty as a gentleman to thank you before I go.

HELENE: *(Quietly.)* Jew.

KARLANNER: *(Stubborn.)* Just like you asked. The end of our private and the beginning of our personal relationship.

HELENE: Jew.

KARLANNER: You keep saying Jew. — So, I thank you.

HELENE: *(Warm.)* You have to go. They're waiting for you.

KARLANNER: *(Hesitates.)* Yes. *(Helene looks through her bookshelves.)*

HELENE: You can get as old as I am and still have no idea.

KARLANNER: Of what?

HELENE: You live your life without a clue and convince yourself you're enlightened. Then suddenly it turns out you're just ignorant. Either way, you're out the door. Out the door here, out the door everywhere. *(She finds a book, sets it aside.)*

KARLANNER: *(Red.)* You're going to read a book?

HELENE: Maybe there's something in it about Judaism.

KARLANNER: Can't you wait till I'm gone?

HELENE: I have a lot of catching up to do.

KARLANNER: *(Pause.)* Well?

HELENE: Well?

KARLANNER: This is good-bye?

HELENE: The good-bye you wanted.

KARLANNER: *(Looks away.)* I thought it would be different.

HELENE: What did you think would happen?

KARLANNER: First, that you would see it my way.

HELENE: *(Motionless.)* I see it now.

KARLANNER: That you'd agree I was right. *(Quietly.)* That I can't be any different.

HELENE: You can't be any different. I see that now.

KARLANNER: Second . . .

HELENE: Say it.

KARLANNER: When I sat in my room, not knowing what would become of me, I'd think of you: She'll find a way out.

HELENE: *(Quietly.)* Not anymore.

KARLANNER: You — a Jew, the cleverest people in the world. You'd find us a way out.

HELENE: I know nothing anymore.

KARLANNER: You say that so calmly. Like you don't want to know anymore.

HELENE: I know nothing, Peter.

KARLANNER: Nothing.

HELENE: There's a storm breaking all over Germany and I know nothing.

KARLANNER: *(Confused.)* So.

HELENE: Did your heart fight for me as long as it could? *(Karlanner controls himself.)* Did your reason? Did your whole self fight for me?

KARLANNER: *(Barely audible.)* My whole self.

HELENE: Your whole, beautiful self.

KARLANNER: *(Mechanically.)* My self.

HELENE: A huge storm . . . and we're like leaves. Weak, helpless, lost. Both of us. *(Karlanner touches his forehead on her forehead.)* We must let it blow over us. At least we can know it's not our fault. There's comfort in that. It's not our fault.

KARLANNER: It's not.

HELENE: It's getting closer and closer. For you three generals, and for me a book.

KARLANNER: *(Afraid.)* So?

HELENE: Take care of yourself. Don't drink too much. You can't take it.

KARLANNER: *(Choking.)* So?

HELENE: *(Gives him coat and hat from the chair. Half-loud.)* But we can see each other once in a while?

KARLANNER: *(Nods.)* So. *(Karlanner bows to her, exits. Helene sits down, holding the book.)*

HELENE: It's not our fault.

RED HERRING
Michael Hollinger

Red Herring is a love story/mystery set in 1952. James and Lynn, both in their twenties, have been watching the Army/McCarthy hearings on the TV.

LYNN: James!

JAMES: You want to take a walk?

LYNN: A walk?

JAMES: Since the leaves are so pretty.

LYNN: Sure, after the hearings are over . . . *(She reaches to turn up the sound, but he takes her hand.)*

JAMES: I guess I just wanted a chance to be alone.

LYNN: We're alone.

JAMES: Without your mom in the next room.

LYNN: She won't bother us; she's on the phone with my Aunt Pidge. *(Beat.)*

JAMES: Well . . . all right. *(She reaches for the TV, but he grabs her hand and reaches into his pocket.)*

LYNN: James?

JAMES: Here. *(He pulls out a small box and places it in her hand.)*

LYNN: What is . . . *(She opens it.)* Oh my goodness.

JAMES: Do you like it?

LYNN: It's beautiful!

JAMES: It's real.

LYNN: And so big . . . !

JAMES: That's what I asked for, "Gimme something big," I said, " 'Cause I got a great big love for this little lady."

LYNN: Oh, Bunny . . . *(She kisses him on the cheek.)*

JAMES: Hey, don't waste that kiss on my cheek! *(She smiles and kisses him on the mouth.)*

LYNN: Let's go show Mother . . .

JAMES: Hold on — read the inscription.

LYNN: "One plus one equals . . . *(She turns the ring sideways.)* eight"?

JAMES: It's an infinity symbol.

LYNN: Oh!

JAMES: Because our love is infinite.

LYNN: I knew that didn't add up to eight.

JAMES: Let's see how it looks on you. *(He puts the ring on her finger.)*

LYNN: My heart's racing . . .

JAMES: You should have seen the jeweler's face when I said it was for Joe McCarthy's daughter.

LYNN: Did he say something mean?

JAMES: Heck no, you kidding? He gave me a discount! Though it was still pretty steep — you know, with all those carats . . . There!

LYNN: Oh, it's just perfect . . .

JAMES: So, you . . . really like it, then . . . ?

LYNN: Of course, silly, you know I do.

JAMES: I mean, you know what I mean. Do you . . . will you . . . ?

LYNN: Of course, silly, you know I will!

JAMES: Shazam!

LYNN: Now can we show Mother?

JAMES: Not so fast . . .

LYNN: Bunny!

JAMES: There's something I need to talk about first.

LYNN: I know what you're going to say.

JAMES: I don't think so.

LYNN: As long as you convert in time for the wedding, my parents will never be the wiser.

JAMES: Convert?

LYNN: Well you can't expect me to be Jewish, I'm Irish.

JAMES: Neither one of us should have to convert.

LYNN: You don't believe in God as it is, what difference would it make to be Catholic?

JAMES: Let's not get into this now. I really need to tell you something.

LYNN: Okay, okay, then tell me. *(Beat.)*

JAMES: You'll really marry me?

LYNN: Didn't I just say so?

JAMES: I know, but . . . *(Beat.)*

LYNN: But what, what do you have to tell me?

JAMES: Um, this should come as a bit of a surprise . . .

LYNN: If it's anything like your last surprise, it's okay by me. What is it? *(Beat.)* James? *(Beat.)*

JAMES: I'm a spy. *(Pause.)*

LYNN: Excuse me?

JAMES: I said I'm a —

LYNN: What do you mean you're a spy?

JAMES: I mean I'm a Soviet spy. *(Pause.)*

LYNN: So that's what you do all the time in New Mexico?

JAMES: Not . . . all the time, but —

LYNN: I've been telling everyone you're a physicist.

JAMES: Well, I am —

LYNN: But you're really a spy?

JAMES: Not so loud . . .

LYNN: Bunny, that is so glamorous . . . *(Pause.)*

JAMES: You mean you don't mind?

LYNN: Are you kidding? Wait'll I tell Daddy . . .

JAMES: Uh, you can't tell your father.

LYNN: Why not?

JAMES: 'Cause it's a secret.

LYNN: Well you told me.

JAMES: You're my fiancée.

LYNN: Where do you find them?

JAMES: Find what?

LYNN: Soviets. In the desert.

JAMES: Uh . . .

LYNN: They should send you to Moscow, more of them there;

JAMES: Well —

LYNN: . . . though I wouldn't want to move to Moscow, would you? So cold and gloomy . . .

JAMES: I don't spy on Soviets.

LYNN: You've said New Mexico's nice, though . . .

JAMES: Did you hear he?

LYNN: What.

JAMES: I said I don't spy on Soviets. *(Beat.)*

LYNN: I don't understand.

JAMES: I don't spy *on* them. I spy for them. *(Pause.)*

LYNN: You mean you're a Commie?

JAMES: Well, I don't go to meetings, but —

LYNN: Oh my God, you're a Commie!

JAMES: Shhh . . .

LYNN: COMMIE!

JAMES: Lynn . . .

LYNN: COMMIE!

JAMES: Sorry. I didn't mean to drop it on you like that.

LYNN: Why are you a Commie?

JAMES: I'm not —

LYNN: You just told me —

JAMES: *I'm not a Commie.* I just think . . . *(He gathers his thoughts.)* Down there in the desert, we're building a bomb. A super-bomb, so powerful no nation in the world should keep it to themselves, even us. So, I've been passing information to the Russians so they can build one for themselves.

LYNN: I thought they already had the Bomb.

JAMES: The atom bomb's only a fission bomb — neutrons splitting other atoms. But the Super is a fusion bomb — neutrons joining other atoms.

LYNN: So this one will kill people deader than the other?

JAMES: The point is not to kill anyone, the point — if only one man has a gun, then everyone else is in danger. But if two men each have a gun, there's a balance of power, so we all stay safe.

LYNN: Unless they both decide to shoot us. *(James considers this wisdom for a second, then brushes it aside:)*

JAMES: Look, I don't want to argue; I want you to be my wife. So we'll never have to argue again.

LYNN: All right, but you have to stop this spy business.

JAMES: I will.

LYNN: Promise.

JAMES: I promise.

LYNN: Good. *(They kiss.)*

JAMES: . . . after I deliver this one last package —

LYNN: James!

JAMES: . . . the last set of blueprints before we test.

LYNN: No.

JAMES: It's simple.

LYNN: I said no.

JAMES: . . . a ten-second hand-off in Boston next Friday.

LYNN: You won't even be in the country by then.

JAMES: I know.

LYNN: You'll be in the middle of the ocean!

JAMES: I know.

LYNN: Then how do you expect to deliver a package in Bost*oh God you want me to do it . . .*

JAMES: It'll be so easy.

LYNN: Oh God, James . . .

JAMES: Just tell your mom you're visiting friends at Radcliffe . . .

LYNN: I can't believe this . . .

JAMES: It's totally anonymous.

LYNN: First you tell me you're a Commie . . .

JAMES: I'm not a . . .

LYNN: Then you want me to be a Commie . . .

JAMES: I'm only asking you —

LYNN: Commie!

JAMES: Don't call me that.

LYNN: Commie!

JAMES: Shh — Lynn!

LYNN: COMMIE COMMIE COMMIE COMMIE COMMIE —
    (*James moves swiftly behind Lynn, covering her mouth with his right hand.*)

SIGNATURE
Beth Henley

This comedy takes place in The Future. Maxwell (thirties), is distraught because his wife, L-Tip, has divorced him via video. He has decided to be a martyr to twenty-first century romantic love by calling the Euthanasia Hot Line, requesting to be "euthed." Here, L-Tip is interviewing Max on television.

> *Satellite station. The Celeb Bites' theme music plays. L-Tip is interviewing Max on Celeb Bites. Max wears his charm suit and turban. He looks the perfect lost poet. L-Tip wears a dress made of different colored eyeglasses. She has green eyeglasses painted around her eyes. Her persona is that of the highly sexual intellectual. They both wear heavy makeup. A bright pink light burns down on them. The theme music dies down. L-Tip smiles into the camera.*

L-TIP: Welcome to *Celeb Bites.* I'm L-Tip the Hip Lip, your guest host. Tonight we are chewing it up with poet Maxwell T-Thorp, the man who is going to euth himself for love. Is he a romantic hero or a cowardly imbecile? Let's find out. Hello, Max.

MAXWELL: Hello, L-Tip.

L-TIP: So, tell us, Max, how long do you have?

MAXWELL: It's just a matter of completing the paperwork.

L-TIP: I hear the paperwork's appalling.

MAXWELL: Yes. Dreadful. It could take . . . who knows?

L-TIP: Well, you fascinate me, M. T-Thorp. Tell us your story. How did you ever reach this point of desperation?

MAXWELL: I, well, I met her when we were very young. We went to school together. She'd sit at her terminal and make little cooing sounds. At recess one day she shared her soyball sandwich with me. Later we were married. I got a job at the Tank Bureau. I had half a cubicle, access to coffee dot, a key to the M. room, all your basic extra features. Then she divorced me. That's when I discovered, love can kill you.

L-TIP: And yet you sit here, looking very zog. Your poems are today's craze. The laser show's in the works. I mean, aren't you being peculiarly short-eyed? Things change very rab in this world. Why you could find a new love tomorrow. Or perhaps even tonight.

MAXWELL: I don't think so. You see, I'm not one of your twenty-first century use and cruisers who dispose of love like it was last meal's fuel frock.

L-TIP: Yet couldn't it be argued that you are wasting a life that should be cherished by committing this cowardly act of self-aggrandizement?

MAXWELL: I don't see that I'm wasting my life. In fact, just the opposite. Certainly to go on living would be the real coward's play. But I refuse to desecrate my profound love by adhering to the notion that it can be replaced, or forgotten, or lived without. I believe by dying I'm tipping my hat to life and the grand effect it can have on the living.

L-TIP: I'm sorry to say this but listening to you, I don't think you have any idea what real love is. Why, if you understood mature love, you would come to love and accept yourself and not degenerate into this destructive, distorted, masochistic indulgence.

MAXWELL: Yes, I'm afraid it's true. I don't know what real or mature love is. It's a mystery to me as I believe it is to most human beings. But the glorious thing is I dove instinctively into the splatter, having no idea how to swim, and now I'm going down for the third count and I have no regrets; the water is green and cool and I would rather be here than standing endlessly alone on the parched, dry shore.

L-TIP: I don't understand you. You never even treated her that well. This woman. I — I've done my research. And you pogoed around. You always pogoed around. You forgot her birthday eleven times. You ignored her at parties. You complained about the meals she clicked. You tore the arms off her Chee Chee Kitty.

MAXWELL: All the more reason. All the more reason to salvage the remnants of a love I shattered through reckless abuse.

L-TIP: But there you are again, only thinking of yourself. Why, she wouldn't want — any of this.

MAXWELL: How do you know?

L-TIP: I — she — we've talked.

MAXWELL: Yes. And what does she want?

L-TIP: She doesn't want you to euth yourself. She — she would take you back. If you did not do that.

MAXWELL: But does she . . . ? Is she . . . ? Could she love me still?

L-TIP: I — don't know. Things are so different. Everything.

MAXWELL: I can't go back without it. Always hoping for its return like sawed-off legs that will never grow back. Please. Tell me. What?

L-TIP: I — how can I? It's — you'll have to ask her.

MAXWELL: There's nothing to ask.

L-TIP: You're a charlatan. You're just doing this to sell your book. You'll call it off before it's over. *(To the camera:)* M.'s and M.'s that is my prediction.

MAXWELL: I understand your stupidity. You can't help it. You don't know her. The woman, I love. She's like no one else. She cries blue tears. *(They look at each other silently. We hear the sound of distant thunder as the lights fade.)*

SOMETHING IN THE AIR
Richard Dresser

Both Sloane and Walker are thirty to forty. In this scene Walker, who has been observing Sloane in a restaurant, makes a move on her.

Lights up on Sloane alone at a table in a restaurant, dressed for a glamorous night out. She sips a martini, then smiles and gestures in the direction of the bar. Walker comes to her table, a bottle of beer in hand.

SLOANE: Are you the one?

WALKER: The one what?

SLOANE: I was supposed to meet someone here. But you seem to be someone else.

WALKER: I am someone else. But I'd be willing to meet you here.

SLOANE: But you're not the one. I saw you over at the bar in your cashmere coat.

WALKER: Actually it's Vect-O-Lene. Comes in a variety of lively colors and it's reversible.

SLOANE: *(Touches it.)* Nice. There you were, drinking your beer and stealing glances in my direction.

WALKER: I couldn't take my eyes off you. You're very well assembled.

SLOANE: I don't like sitting by myself. I'm afraid of what I might do.

WALKER: I've got a solution. I could sit down. *(He sits down with Sloane.)*

SLOANE: You don't even have to talk. We could sit here in silence.

WALKER: Except people might think we were married.

SLOANE: My name is Sloane.

WALKER: Walker. Whoever stood you up is insane.

SLOANE: Perhaps it's unavoidable. Sometimes a person will get off a bus and just disappear into thin air.

WALKER: That's very rare. Anyway, *I'd* avoid it. I wouldn't leave a beautiful woman sitting here all alone. If I were that other guy I'd get here early so a guy like me wouldn't get swept off his feet and decide he'll do whatever it takes to get you away from me, if I were that other guy.

SLOANE: You don't know me from a gaping hole in your head.

WALKER: I'll worm my way into your life. You'll think I've gone but I'll be creepy-crawling toward you in the dark. That guy doesn't stand a chance and neither do you.

SLOANE: Would it change anything if I told you I was a prostitute?

WALKER: It's the weekend. Let's not talk about work.

SLOANE: You're pretty sure of yourself, aren't you?

WALKER: I'm onto a sure thing. I'm coming into bucks. I'd like to celebrate with a moist kiss.

SLOANE: You and what army? This wasn't a good idea. He'll get upset when he sees you sitting there salivating.

WALKER: I'll coldcock him. I'll rattle his brains. He'll go down hard.

SLOANE: Jesus, don't say that! Anger terrifies me. My father used to get angry.

WALKER: Everyone gets angry.

SLOANE: Not like my father. Once he was so angry his face turned red and it looked as if his head would explode and then . . .

WALKER: What?

SLOANE: No. It's too awful. I couldn't.

WALKER: Tell me.

SLOANE: Oh, all right, if you insist. But it isn't pretty. Something flew out of his ear and landed on the floor. It made a clicking sound as it hit the linoleum.

WALKER: What was it?

SLOANE: A glistening gray orb, trembling slightly. We left it where it landed. The next morning my brother found it in the vestibule. It had moved in the night, pulsing with its own savage energy.

WALKER: Whatever did you do with it?

SLOANE: My brother put it in a shoe box under his bed. It was a monstrously hot summer, and there it stayed, week after languid week. One night my brother heard a tap-tapping so we got a flashlight and looked under the bed and the top of the shoe box was moving up and down, tapping against the wall.

WALKER: You don't see that very often.

SLOANE: We bound the top with string and put it back under the bed. In the morning, the shoe box had moved to the center of the room and the string was broken and as we watched, paralyzed, the top of the box lifted and a single rheumy eye was staring back at us.

WALKER: Good God.

SLOANE: Really. So we ran from the room and I sat at the piano for hours playing with great ferocity and I could see my brother sitting cross-legged on the lawn, just staring with this stunned and shattered look. I was supposed to go off to school the next week. My brother begged me not to leave him all alone with that disturbing thing in the shoe box.

WALKER: Did you leave. *(Beat.)* It's understandable. You can't get anywhere without an education.

SLOANE: Thanksgiving, when I saw my brother, he smiled at me in such a peculiar way that I knew in my heart my poor brother had met some hideous end and this being who looked like my brother was really the awful creature from the shoe box. *(Beat.)* Do you believe me?

WALKER: Of course I believe you. I've had similar experiences. Well, kind of similar.

SLOANE: Why didn't I stay and protect my brother?

WALKER: We've all done things we aren't proud of.

SLOANE: I'm sorry I told you that story. We had lots of good times in our family, too.

WALKER: I have to see you again.

SLOANE: No. My rule is, I only see men for one date. Any more than that is just asking for trouble.

WALKER: But this wasn't my date. This was a chance meeting.

(Sloane considers as the lights fade.)

STRANGER
Craig Lucas

Hush, probably thirties and Diane, early twenties, relive a scene that may have happened years ago, involving a sadistic kidnapping.

> *A cabin in the woods. Hush lights a gas lamp; he is younger. Also there is Diane. She speaks with a North Carolina accent.*

DIANE: Cool. Wow.

HUSH: You like something to drink?

DIANE: Sure. What do you have?

HUSH: I have some beer.

DIANE: Beer's fine.

HUSH: You were drinking, what was it?

DIANE: Lillet?

HUSH: Don't have any of that.

DIANE: That's all right. Honestly? Any beer is fine.

HUSH: So your family . . . ?

DIANE: You have a really intense energy, you know that? When you were at the bar, even with your back to me, I could feel . . . some people just have . . . something . . . crackling, like a power station. You do. In spades! Heat, electricity, magnetism, ego. Honestly.
   (Pause.)

HUSH: You, too.

DIANE: Thanks. Yeah, my family. Ummmm, they're kind of a titular family, if you know what I mean . . . Family only nominally speaking . . . In appearance only, I mean, yeah. I left home at fifteen and haven't seen them, only spoke to my mom a couple of times.

HUSH: Really?

DIANE: Yeah. Annnd, this is pretty, your place, it's wild . . . Good place to write.

HUSH: Go on.

DIANE: Uhhh, that's what I love about strangers . . . If you sit in a coffee shop and watch people walk by or listen in to their conversations at the other table, or meet somebody . . . like this . . . No history, all fresh clean blank slate . . . chance . . . promise, —

HUSH: Uh-huh.

DIANE: — possibility. I love that. Mystery. Danger. Romance. *(Pause.)* It's neat.

HUSH: It is.

DIANE: Honestly? First thing, when I looked at you, I thought, "Wait a minute, there's something — " What? *(Pause.)* Are you hearing something? . . . What?

HUSH: That . . . There . . . little . . . in there —

DIANE: Oh, yeah.

HUSH: I gotta tighten that.

DIANE: You do your own plumbing?

HUSH: Well, sure.

DIANE: Of course.

HUSH: Who else is gonna —

DIANE: You would. Back to . . . back to nature. So what's your book about?

HUSH: Oh, it's not good . . .

DIANE: Oh? I —

HUSH: . . . to give too much away before . . . you . . .

DIANE: The creative process.

HUSH: Yeah, so . . .

DIANE: Is it your first novel?

HUSH: Maybe this wasn't such a good idea, you know.

DIANE: What? . . . You mean . . .

HUSH: My stomach.

DIANE: Oh, are you not feeling well?

HUSH: Maybe . . . It's o — . . . It's okay.

DIANE: Well, I can't . . . You'd have to drive. I can't walk all the way back to New Hope, it's, how long is it?

HUSH: It's okay. I . . . That *noise.*

DIANE: I . . . I barely hear it, honestly.

HUSH: Why do you keep saying that? "Honestly." "Honestly."
(Pause.)

DIANE: Yeah, you should drive me back. I'm sorry.

HUSH: It's okay. I've got to take a whiz.

DIANE: Sure. Then . . . ?

(Hush goes into the bathroom. Pause. Finally he emerges.)

HUSH: Sorry, I'm —

DIANE: It's okay.

HUSH: I wrote and wrote and wrote, two days straight. I haven't slept.

DIANE: I understand.

HUSH: Sorry.

DIANE: It's okay.

HUSH: You're very pretty.

DIANE: Well. *(Pause.)* Thank you. *(Pause.)* You . . . we should go.

HUSH: Yes. Sorry.

DIANE: It's fine.

HUSH: . . . I shouldn't . . .

DIANE: It's really okay.

(Pause.)

HUSH: Okay.

DIANE: Some other time.

HUSH: Some other time.

DIANE: Let's —

HUSH: May I . . . kiss you?

DIANE: Oh. I don't, yes, sure . . .

HUSH: Is it . . . ?

DIANE: Okay.

(Pause. They kiss.)

DIANE: Mmmm. Mmmmm. I feel . . . What's that? You're trying to . . . change my mind. Unh-unh.

HUSH: No, I'm not. Let's go.

DIANE: Okay. *(Pause.)* Okay.

HUSH: What?

DIANE: You're just a little boy, aren't you? . . . Okay.

HUSH: Go ahead.

(She starts toward the door and he overpowers her, handcuffing her wrist to her ankle; as they struggle:)

DIANE: What are you doing? Get off! No. Please. Please, oh please don't do this. Hush, don't, I'm your friend — I swear, I won't tell anyone, let me go, please — Help! Please don't please don't hurt me, please, don't hurt me. Goddamn you — Help! HELP! Help me. Somebody help!

(He has at last wrestled her into the trunk, shut her inside. Long pause. Dissolve back into the present: Linda's cabin. She is making tea for Hush and herself.)

LINDA: Was there any part of it that was . . . thrilling? That —

HUSH: Yes.

LINDA: There was. Thank you. I want to understand. How you got from one place . . . The place I understand . . . where their eyes are pleading and your own heart is pounding . . where their life is in your hands . . .

HUSH: I could do anything, she belonged to me.

LINDA: Yes. He belonged to me. His existence. He was . . .

HUSH: Yeah.

LINDA: An object.

HUSH: A thing.

(Pause.)

LINDA: We're alike . . . in . . . the first half of our stories . . . but . . . how do you acquit yourself?

(She brings him his tea.)

HUSH: Thanks.

LINDA: Forgive yourself, I mean. It's herbal.

HUSH: Christ.

LINDA: I hope that's okay.

HUSH: Christ does. Christ takes care of all of it.

LINDA: It has no caffeine, it'll help you sleep. *(Pause.)* This . . . I don't know, this might . . . I mean, I didn't — I had nothing against Frank, he pissed me off sometimes, but . . . you couldn't hate Frank, there was nothing to hate, there wasn't — I liked him . . . I, I mean, did you like her . . . ? The girl? D'you talk to each other? You must've. *(Pause.)* In all that time? . . . *(Pause.)* Did you hate her? . . .

HUSH: Why am I here?

LINDA: I . . . Whhh — ?

HUSH: Where's the other bed?

LINDA: Oh.

HUSH: You said there were —

LINDA: Up in the attic, you can help me bring it down, it's a cot . . . I forgot I put it up there, you want to get it now? We can. *(Pause.)* You're . . . I hope . . . you're here to help me. Aren't you? *(Pause.)* You said you wanted to help people. The way you'd been helped. Find . . . Didn't you? . . . All I want is to understand.

HUSH: Understanding is the booby prize. The peace that passeth all understanding. You ever hear that. *(Pause.)* Hey.

LINDA: Hey.

HUSH: Give me the pills. The ones you were going to take.

LINDA: Oh.

HUSH: I don't want you swallowing them after I go to sleep which could make me accessory to a crime.

LINDA: *(Giving him her pills.)* I guess it's something you have to think about. I can't even imagine. *(Short pause.)* Why'd you pick her? I mean, I know, the voices, but . . . what was it about her? *(Pause.)* If this is too difficult. Did you feel sorry for her? Did you think she deserved to die?

HUSH: That isn't the way it was.

LINDA: Well . . . was she the kind of woman, I mean, would you have dated her? In other . . . What?

HUSH: Date. It's such a funny word.

LINDA: Why? *(Pause.)* Didn't you ever date people?

HUSH: By the time I was in high school, I barely spoke . . .

LINDA: Uh-huh.

HUSH: — to people; I wouldn't let them near me, I'd say as little as possible and move away.

LINDA: What about . . . earlier? *(Pause.)* You've always been alone.

HUSH: . . . Earlier's the place I never go.

LINDA: . . . Why?

HUSH: It's too good. It's like another life. Somebody else's.

LINDA: Then . . . I would think you'd like to remember that . . . Wouldn't you?

HUSH: Why? So I could remind myself I can't have it.

LINDA: Why can't you have it? . . . Can't you try again?

HUSH: Try what? Be eight again? Be tucked in, be told things, and believe; be kissed; I'm not feeling sorry for myself, I'm being honest. I
won't be. I won't believe, I won't be kissed.

LINDA: Why?

(Pause.)

HUSH: I'm trying to tell you. *(Silence.)* I want to strike out, I have urges.

LINDA: People want to do things all the time — steal things, kill people,
burn . . . buildings. That's . . . It's human. That doesn't mean they . . .
are compelled. There's a difference between feelings and actions.

HUSH: Then you don't have to kill yourself.

LINDA: And you don't have to strike out.

(Pause.)

HUSH: You don't understand.

LINDA: No.

HUSH: All the things . . . If I think, and I don't, I promise you, when these
thoughts come up, I let them go: I refuse to follow them back to . . .
(Pause.)

LINDA: Where?

HUSH: Oh . . . washing the car with my dad, tickled, being tickled by my
sister, you're trying to trick me, aren't you? School, haircuts, school
projects . . . A book on transportation: all cut out pictures from magazines and pasted on construction paper? That was a kind of . . .
bliss — I start to look back on that, and . . .

LINDA: What?

HUSH: Rips my heart out of my chest. My family'd . . . they have in-
junctions out against me, they'd never take me back. Burying me is
easier than looking at me.

LINDA: Make your own family.

(Pause.)

HUSH: Yeah. I can't even see myself in a picture with other people . . .
without destroying them.

(Pause.)

LINDA: That's why you have to save them. *(Pause.)* That's just a fear.
(Pause.) Did anybody ever come around after you'd . . . ? I mean,
checking on you or her, what was her name?

HUSH: Diane.

LINDA: Scream?

HUSH: . . . She stopped after a few days.

LINDA: Screaming? . . . What was that like . . . ? . . . listening to that?

HUSH: Like a gnawing, an agony . . . sort of like when a little baby screams and screams and nothing you can do will stop it, you want to hit it finally, shut it up. I liked it, too, because it was my "god" saying, Kill her, go ahead, put her out of this pain, do it now. Now! Hurry up . . . Save the universe. Save mankind. Join her to *us*. *(Pause.)* Finally she stopped. *(Silence.)* . . . I'd come home from . . . looking for food . . . panhandling. She hardly ever spoke to me after those first few days. Nothing for a long time. What?

LINDA: I was going to make a joke. In bad taste, "Some women are just so touchy. Put 'em in a trunk and they freeze you out." You're right . . . Bad devil! Down. Go on. Sorry.

HUSH: You're nuts.

LINDA: Oh, the kettle speaks about the other kitchen appliances. *I'm* nuts. So, I'm Satan, I can't help it, I'm trying to work on myself, cut me some slack. I'm in therapy!

HUSH: You make jokes about everything.

LINDA: That's how I survive. I'll try not to make so many jokes, all right, that's the best I can do is try. *(Short pause.)* I'll *try.*
(Hush places a chair in the middle of the room.)

HUSH: Try to move that chair.

LINDA: What?

HUSH: Try to move this chair. *(Pause.)* Try.

LINDA: Move it where?

HUSH: Anywhere. Try to move it an inch.

LINDA: Are you . . . ? What, are you hyper kinetic or something? You can control objects? *(She pretends she can't budge the chair.)* No, I can't move it. Oh my god! You *are* Satan!
(She moves the chair.)

HUSH: Uhn-uhn. I said try. You moved it. I said "*Try* to move it."

LINDA: Oh. I see. What did I say . . . ?

HUSH: You said you were gonna try to stop making jokes.

LINDA: Ah, yes.

HUSH: That's like trying to quit smoking. Anybody tells you they're trying to quit ain't gonna do it. Doing and trying to do are two different things. One's a lie. It's like when your parents say "Maybe." It's a lie, means no. If you're gonna try to stop doing something, you're not gonna stop. If you're doing something, you're not trying, you're doing it. You either accept Jesus or you don't, it's no more complicated than that.

LINDA: Just . . . say the words.

HUSH: No, that's like trying. Just mean the words.

LINDA: Mean the words. I accept Jesus into my heart, I accept Jesus into my heart.

HUSH: There you go.

LINDA: I, Linda Asnitz, accept Jesus into my heart. I invite him in, I accept him, I . . . embrace —

HUSH: That's enough, it'll do. *(Pause.)* How do you feel?
    (A shrug. Pause.)

LINDA: I still want to know how you fought for a year, against . . . People usually do something or they don't, isn't that what you were just saying? They don't try not to do it, I agree with you.
    (Pause.)

HUSH: You didn't kill . . .

LINDA: Frank?

HUSH: Frank.

LINDA: I didn't want to. I wanted to humiliate him. If I'd wanted to kill him, I could have gotten away with it. Otherwise . . . You must have wanted something else from her. Diane.

HUSH: Like?

LINDA: You tell me. *(Silence.)* What stopped you? . . . What were your voices saying?, what did you hear? Exactly, can you tell me?

TRUDY BLUE
Marsha Norman

James and Ginger are both thirties to forties. Ginger is a successful writer who has recently found that she has terminal cancer. Here she is sharing some quality time with James, who may just possibly be a figment of her imagination.

James appears in the hotel room wearing a white terry bathrobe.

JAMES: The Jacuzzi is great. You should try it.

GINGER: I don't want to get my hair wet.

JAMES: They have a dryer.

GINGER: I don't want to dry my hair. I want to not get it wet. *(Then recovering.)* Maybe this wasn't a good idea.

JAMES: This was a great idea.

(James opens his arms and she walks into them. He begins to rub her back.)

GINGER: I can't stay long.

JAMES: Are you afraid of what would happen if you didn't have to leave?

GINGER: Probably. *(A moment.)* I'm afraid of a lot of things these days.

JAMES: Like the jacuzzi? Or are you just avoiding me?

GINGER: *(A little irritated.)* I'm avoiding having a bath.

JAMES: Why?

GINGER: Because it will make me want you.

JAMES: And you don't want me?

[*(There is a knock at the door.)*

TRUDY: Room Service.

JAMES: Saved by the bell. *(Trudy enters. Ginger is not happy to see her.)*

GINGER: We don't need you here, Trudy.

TRUDY: That's what you think.

GINGER: Yes. That's what I think.

(Trudy leaves.)]

(James offers a toast.)

JAMES: To us. To happiness.

GINGER: To happily ever after?

JAMES: That sounds good.

GINGER: Nobody ever lived happily ever after. If we had a shred of courage, we'd tell our children the truth.

JAMES: Talk to me, Ginger.

GINGER: I want time to stop. It doesn't have to be for long. I just want one week with you where I don't have to work or worry or plan anything or remember anything or call anybody, or anything.

JAMES: Where would you like to go?

GINGER: I need to get myself together somehow. I just don't know how. I don't know whether to check into a motel or a monastery.

JAMES: How about a monastery where you could get laid?

GINGER: *(Laughs.)* Perfect. Do you have their number?

JAMES: If you're serious, I could go week after next.

GINGER: I can't go anywhere. I don't actually want to go anywhere. I don't want to want anything. I want to be a Buddhist.

JAMES: It's a peaceful life they say.

GINGER: You're no help. You're agreeing with whatever I say.

JAMES: I'm trying to help. But you think it's all impossible.

GINGER: Is that what I think? That's not what I think about you, is it?

JAMES: Well of course not. But that's because I'm perfect.

GINGER: *(Laughs, teasing him.)* You're not perfect.

JAMES: I'm not? Then tell me something that's not perfect about me.

GINGER: *(Giving in, flirting.)* All right. You're perfect. You're the man of my dreams.

JAMES: That's right. I am. But that doesn't mean there isn't someone out there who —

GINGER: What do you mean, someone out there?

JAMES: A real man who could —

GINGER: A real man? What are *you,* a ghost?

JAMES: More like a wish.

(A long moment.)

GINGER: *(Quietly.)* Oh no.

JAMES: A longing. A need.

GINGER: Please don't let this be true. You're not real. *(He doesn't answer.)* You're in my mind.

JAMES: Ginny, Ginny, the things in your mind are as real as everything else.

(Ginger is stricken almost dumb with sadness and despair.)

GINGER: I can't spend the night with you? I can't wake up next to you?

JAMES: I thought you knew.

GINGER: *(Her fury beginning to burn.)* I knew I was lonely. I didn't know I was *this* lonely. How did this happen? Were you real in the beginning?

JAMES: You called me. We met in the bar.

GINGER: We talked about Morocco, we met for drinks a couple of times. And then you said something I had been praying somebody would say to me someday, and suddenly, you were the one. The perfect man. You knew what I needed. You knew how to love me. And before I knew it, I was dreaming about you all night, and talking to you all day. *(A moment.)* But it wasn't you. I wasn't talking to you. *(Throws something.)* I was talking to my idea of you, my idea of what would make me happy.

JAMES: Ginny. Don't be —

GINGER: I have two months to live! I can't spend it with somebody I made up!

(He comes to her, but she moves away from him.)

GINGER: My life is done.

JAMES: You need to cry for yourself.

GINGER: I need to go home.

JAMES: Just let me hold you.

GINGER: I have to say good-bye to the people I really had, James, not the people I wish I had.

(He holds out his arms to her. She looks at him, but doesn't move.)

GINGER: I don't know what to do with my wishes.

U.S. DRAG
Gina Gionfriddo

Both characters are in their twenties. Christopher has written a very successful book about his horrible childhood. Angela, a recent college graduate, is looking for ways to make a lot of money, in a very short time, with little or no effort.

Christopher Collins' hotel room. He looks like he hasn't slept in years and just crawled out of bed.

CHRISTOPHER: My parents sent me a telegram in Boston: Read book (stop) Wish you would die (stop) So we could live again (stop) You're dead to us now (stop) Good-bye (stop) *(Pause.)* I called my sponsor, he said: "If you ever doubted that you are a victim — of toxic parenting of the most virulent kind . . ." I mean you don't send a telegram like that to someone with as many problems as I have, right? You just don't.

ANGELA: That really sucks.

CHRISTOPHER: I'm lucky to be alive. I'm lucky to be sitting here right now. What I've been through — I should be DEAD. I'm sorry — What's your name again?

ANGELA: Angela.

CHRISTOPHER: Angela. I'm at the top of my career. I have a *New York Times* Notable Book. I was interviewed in *Time* and *Newsweek.* This should be the happiest time of my life and all I do is cry. The people who brought me into this world want me dead. How am I supposed to process that?

ANGELA: We could raid your mini bar.

CHRISTOPHER: I don't drink. *(Pause.)* I probably shouldn't put this all on you but . . . you know. You're the only one here.

ANGELA: Right . . . How about if just I raid your mini bar?

CHRISTOPHER: I'd rather you didn't. *(Pause.)* Do you have any cigarettes?

ANGELA: Yes.

CHRISTOPHER: You remind me of my sister. My sister smokes five packs of cigarettes a day and lives in a trailer. She cuts hair. She's almost as smart as I am and she's cutting fucking hair. My parents did that. They beat the spirit out of her. They spiritually murdered her. And now they want me.

ANGELA: They definitely sound like assholes.

CHRISTOPHER: I should give you something. For being so nice to me and letting me bum your cigarettes. I should give you something.

ANGELA: OK. You can give me something. Great.

CHRISTOPHER: Have you read my book?

ANGELA: No.

CHRISTOPHER: I'm gonna give you one. *(Pause.)*
Is that really weird? Was that a bad thing to say? Now do you think I'm like really full of myself because I offered you my book?

ANGELA: What?

CHRISTOPHER: I'm going to give you one. I'll sign it for you.

ANGELA: Great. Is it valuable now?

CHRISTOPHER: Well . . . collectible. Because there's a finite number of copies in the first printing —

ANGELA: Collectible like worth money?

CHRISTOPHER: Well, only if I die.

ANGELA: Then how much?

CHRISTOPHER: I love your demeanor. Your black humor, your quiet irony. It's really sexy. *(Pause.)* Was that really inappropriate to say? Did I just really, really fuck things up?

ANGELA: How much is it worth if you just get hurt?

CHRISTOPHER: You're amazing. I'm gonna write that. To . . . shit I abused myself so bad. I lost brain cells. I can't believe this —

ANGELA: Angela.

CHRISTOPHER: Angela. Sorry. You have to understand I did *everything.* Before I got sober, I did everything. In big, huge disgusting quantities. I went to counseling they were like "you should be dead." I was the worst they'd ever had.

ANGELA: *Breaking the Boy.* Is it a novel?

CHRISTOPHER: It's creative non-fiction.

ANGELA: What does that mean?

CHRISTOPHER: It's my history as I experienced it.

ANGELA: But is it true?

CHRISTOPHER: Truth is an individual construct. If you believe in only one truth, you can believe in only one storyteller. Postmodernism completely exploded that idea, revealed it for what it was — sexist, racist, classist . . . a way to marginalize and/or discount the experiences of certain groups.

ANGELA: So it's . . . not true?

CHRISTOPHER: It's my truth.

ANGELA: What's it about?

CHRISTOPHER: It's about child abuse. Two children, a boy and a girl, enduring unspeakable tortures at the hands of their parents. Somehow, miraculously, they survive. The girl becomes a hairdresser and the boy becomes a writer.

ANGELA: Wow. Your parents abused you?

CHRISTOPHER: Symbolically. What they did to my mind, my soul . . . burning me with cigarettes would have been a relief.

ANGELA: Why do they want you dead?

CHRISTOPHER: There's a scene in the book where my mom blindfolds me and hangs me upside down until I pass out. The spirit of the scene is true. When I didn't make the tennis team, my mom just turned her back and walked out of the room. Hanging upside down in the dark is exactly what that felt like.

ANGELA: So why do they want you dead?

(Pause.)

CHRISTOPHER: I was on the *Today* Show last week. Katie Couric wanted to know if my parents really did that — hung me. She said, "Is that true?" and I said, "Yes, it is." Because it is true. It's my truth. So now my folks are like shunned at the country club or something, I don't know. *(Pause.)* Did that make you uncomfortable?

ANGELA: Which part?

CHRISTOPHER: A movie studio bought my book. They sent me this check which is like more money than my dad made in his whole life. I didn't cash it for a week. I just lay in bed sort of clutching it and crying. Because of my folks. Because I couldn't call them and tell them about it. *(Pause.)* Could we like . . . just lie on the bed and have you hug me?

ANGELA: I guess so.

CHRISTOPHER: I know that's really weird and now you probably hate me and I've ruined everything, but . . . I swear to God I won't touch you. I find sex really frightening, but I haven't slept in three weeks 'cuz my parents want me dead —

ANGELA: Whatever. It's my job. For $6.50 an hour, you know . . . Whatever you want within reason.

CHRISTOPHER: $6.50 an hour? That's horrific. I'll give you some extra if that isn't really crass and offensive.

ANGELA: Not at all. I'm really poor. *(Pause.)* My . . . sister is even . . . poorer.

CHRISTOPHER: Ok, get on the bed. Please don't be frightened.

(Angela lies down on the bed. Christopher gets behind her with two pillows. For a moment it looks as though he might be moving toward smothering her.)

CHRISTOPHER: *(Like a child.)* I like two pillows. *(He gets on the bed and wedges the pillows behind her head. He lies down and "spoons" her aggressively from behind, throwing much of his weight on her body.)* Now let's just sleep like this, OK? Are you OK?

ANGELA: It's pretty uncomfortable . . .

CHRISTOPHER: You smell like powder. You remind me of my baby-sitter. I was never breast-fed.

ANGELA: No?

CHRISTOPHER: That wasn't a come-on, I swear to God. I can't believe I said breast. I'm such an asshole. I fuck everything up.

ANGELA: My neck kinda hurts with you pressing on it like that . . . Wanna sleep on my stomach? I feel like I'm gonna fall off the bed.

(Christopher is snoring. Angela stares at the wall.)

Scenes for
Two Women

AS IT IS IN HEAVEN
Arlene Hutton

As It Is in Heaven takes place in the early nineteenth century, in a Shaker community. The Shakers (founded by a woman, by the way) segregated men and women and disallowed sexual relations. Hannah (thirties to forties) is an "eldress" of the sect. Fanny (twenties) is a young member, who claims to be having visions of angels.

HANNAH: I'm suggesting you leave the community

FANNY: I'm a strong worker. You can't make me leave.

HANNAH: You haven't signed the covenant.

FANNY: When the time comes I'll be a-signin'.

HANNAH: You won't need to.

FANNY: Why wouldn't I? No place better than this. It's heaven on earth here. Learned that from you. Don't you believe that, Sister Hannah?

HANNAH: We are not here to talk about my beliefs, but yours.

FANNY: Is that what we are talking about?

HANNAH: You are insolent.

FANNY: Not meaning to be. Just tryin' to understand.

HANNAH: Then understand that it is time for you to depart.

FANNY: I want to understand the angels. I want to know what they say.

HANNAH: You are making this up.

FANNY: The others hear them. They send them songs. And pictures. I see the angels, but I mostly don't know what they're saying. I want to understand them. I want to know what they say.

HANNAH: Angels speak in heavenly tongues. *(Corrects herself.)* Would speak in heavenly tongues. If they were there.

FANNY: But what do they say? Please help me.

HANNAH: They are not here, I'm telling you.

FANNY: Polly hears them, Izzy hears them. *(She corrects herself.)* Heard them.

HANNAH: You have created this yourself.

FANNY: Why do they talk to me?

HANNAH: Indeed. Why would angels speak to you? *(A pause.)* You must go.

FANNY: Where do you want me to go? You can't just send me away with a little suitcase. No, you wouldn't do that. You care about people. You do, Sister Hannah. You'd be thinking about me. You'd wonder what happened to me. Did my half-wit brother tear my clothes off me in the outhouse? Did I give birth to my father's next child on some snowy night all alone with the wind a-howlin' through the cracks in the windows?

HANNAH: That is enough.

FANNY: You gonna send me out in the cold and pray that I don't end up like Polly a-layin' on my back in some fancy house in Lexington? Some travelin' men a-pawin' at me? Is that where you are sending me? You gonna pray for me there? You gonna pray me to a safe life, or pray that I go quickly to heaven?

HANNAH: You cannot talk to me this way.

FANNY: Won't you even pray for me then? *(Possibly a pause.)*

HANNAH: I pray for you every day.

FANNY: But what do you pray? That I will disappear? Or that I'll show you where the angels are?

HANNAH: We know where you go. The men are clearing the place right now.

FANNY: No!

HANNAH: The land will be plowed and fenced. Perhaps your "angels" won't be there any more. Why don't you simply stop talking about spirits? The others will forget about it and we can all resume our lives here.

FANNY: You're tellin' me that if the angels go away I can stay.

HANNAH: I'm giving you a chance.

FANNY: You're tellin' me that if the angels leave I don't have to.

HANNAH: Girl, think about what you have been doing! Think! Do you honestly believe that celestial manifestations would appear to you, an uneducated young woman who has not even signed the covenant? If Mother Ann were to visit us, don't you think it would be the elders who would see her first? You are not a stupid girl. Don't you think Mother Ann would have something to say to us? To me?

FANNY: Would you recognize her if you saw her?

HANNAH: You will leave tonight!

FANNY: *(With a sudden intake of breath, Fanny looks at something behind Hannah.)* You are not to send me away.

HANNAH: You have no choice.

FANNY: *(Fanny stares at something behind Hannah.)* I'll be good. I try to do . . . I try . . . I try . . .

HANNAH: You will not do this.

FANNY: Don't you see them?

HANNAH: See what? What do you see?

FANNY: They are so beautiful. So beautiful.

HANNAH: *(Hannah looks around.)* There is nothing there.

FANNY: You can't see them, can you? You can't see them.

(Hannah holds Fanny by the shoulders and begins to shake her.)

HANNAH: There is nothing to see.

FANNY: I hear their voices. *(Hannah shakes Fanny.)*

HANNAH: Tell me you see nothing. *(Hannah shakes Fanny harder and harder.)* Tell me you see nothing. Tell me you see nothing! *(She lets go of Fanny and kneels.)* Please. Please. Holy Mother Wisdom, hear my prayer.

FANNY: They speak to me.

HANNAH: Grant me the vision to see from my eyes as well as my heart.

FANNY: *(To her spirits.)* What are you saying? *(Fanny shakes harder and harder and finally collapses on the floor, sobbing joyfully.)*

HANNAH: *(Looking around the room.)* Holy Mother Wisdom, grant me this prayer. Let me see! Let me see! I will see. I will see. You will come to me.

BANG
Laura Shaine Cunningham

Both characters are in their thirties to forties. Sheila and her husband are visiting their old friend Bev, who lives with her new husband in a bomb shelter/condo deep beneath the surface of Utah. Roy, Bev's husband, has just left the room. The two women friends have much to catch up on.

Bev grabs Sheila's hand, pulls her into the bedroom, in high burble.

BEV: Come in the bedroom. We have so much to catch up on. I wanted to talk to you at the wedding . . . really talk . . . but it was so crazy . . . I was in a complete trance . . .

SHEILA: *(More interested in the room.)* What an interesting layout. Len and I need more space . . .

BEV: You wouldn't give up your apartment?

SHEILA: In a second.

BEV: Oh, I always loved your place.

SHEILA: Don't tell Len, but I've made up my mind. We're moving! I'm not going to die in that apartment. I have a plan: Just don't tell Len. You know how he goes on and on about that apartment. *(Bitter tone.)* 4-R. It . . . *(She pokes her head into the bathroom door.)* What's in here? Was this made from some kind of kit?

BEV: A lot of this is prefab.

SHEILA: It looks like an airplane toilet.

BEV: It is. Without the charm. *(Intense whisper.)* Tell me the truth. Was everybody sick of my getting married? Having to buy me gifts every few years?

SHEILA: We just hoped he was the one. *(She is snooping around. With more sincere interest.)* Great storage space.

BEV: The whole place is storage! *(She slides open closet, produces clothing.)* Listen, I put some clothes aside for you . . . if you want them . . .

SHEILA: *(Grabbing a good jacket.)* You're sure? *(She reads the label.)* Bergdorf's? This looks like it was never worn.

BEV: Try the jacket. See if it's long.

(Sheila dons the jacket.)

BEV: God, was that me? It's great on you. I have the sense that I will never need a suit jacket again. You keep it. *(Jubilant whisper.)* I want to tell you something before they come back. You have to promise not to tell.

SHEILA: Who would I tell? I don't talk to anyone.

BEV: Not even Len. Promise . . .

SHEILA: All right. Not even Len.

BEV: *(In low, excited tone.)* Sheila . . . it exists! It can be the way we hoped it would be . . . before we found out . . . it isn't usually that way. *(Pause.)* I had to leave New York to find it. *(Pause.)* He needs a woman several times a day . . . or he gets . . . *(Surprised pause.)* . . . headaches. I don't know if I can tell you this . . . *(Instantly.)* Do you know the *Kama Sutra*?

SHEILA: I don't read that sort of thing.

BEV: We're in it! Roy and I! On the male and female charts. The one that pairs up private parts. We're the highest mating . . . Roy and I!

SHEILA: Please don't describe his organ.

BEV: But it's so pretty! I never thought of one as pretty before . . . but his is! It has a kind of smile. Did you notice the way he walks? *(She struts.)* . . . There's a reason! Everything about it is unique . . . I've never seen one like it . . . and I've looked . . . in magazines. There isn't another with its humor and its, well, dignity. *(She straightens up.)*

SHEILA: Are there a lot of them out there?

BEV: No! He's the only one. Did you think I was crazy to go?

SHEILA: I wouldn't personally pick Death Valley for a vacation . . .

BEV: . . . but it was more than a vacation: It was a test. *(Recalling the trip.)* "Upward Bound" . . . "Fourteen Days to Test Yourself Against the Beauty and Brutality of Nature . . ."

SHEILA: I would have gone to Barbados.

BEV: I needed something . . . different . . . a real change . . . The city was closing in on me . . . You know how it can get? When you see as if through too-strong prescription glasses? The buildings too sharp, and overly outlined? Everything converging? Everybody on the street starts looking moronic . . . their eyes out of kilter . . . *(She makes a moronic face.)* It gets kind of Cubist . . . especially toward summer . . . You don't even want deli anymore. You just don't *care* . . .

SHEILA: *(Thoughtful.)* That's how it was when we left.

(Bev takes a small boulder from the floor, displays it.)

BEV: I saved this rock . . . *(She strokes rock.)* It was near me when I met him.

SHEILA: Bev, it's just a rock.

BEV: Oh, Sheila! You have to understand . . . *(She hands the rock to Sheila.)*

SHEILA: He walks on two feet.

(Bev looks hurt.)

SHEILA: Oh, he's all right. He's great looking.

BEV: All the women on the expedition thought so! You should have seen us hotfooting it across the Mojave . . . Thirteen women from New York . . . all divorced. Sheila, I was *rappelling* after him.

SHEILA: That was dangerous.

BEV: I kept waiting for him to make his move . . . but you know . . . *(She smiles.)* He's really very shy . . .

SHEILA: He doesn't look shy.

BEV: That's a cover-up. He's so shy, I was afraid he'd never do anything. Then . . . it happened. On the solo survival test. I was supposed to go off . . . *alone* . . . for two days . . . to see if I could survive without food or water . . .

SHEILA: Oh my God. What if you can't? Do you get your money back?

BEV: *(Unconcerned.)* Oh, I don't know. I guess you die. I didn't care about that . . . Sheila! Have you ever spent forty-eight hours totally alone outdoors?

SHEILA: I have no desire to . . .

BEV: Oh, you should! It's stupendous. The isolation is supposed to be the hardest part . . . Some people crack up. I just stared at the sky a lot . . . I saw the clouds turn to god men, their beards like cotton candy . . .

SHEILA: Were you hallucinating?

BEV: No, I was hungry. I was supposed to forage, but I just couldn't forage . . . I remembered something Roy taught me, how if you're too weak to hunt, you can attract birds by making kissing sounds on the back of your hand . . . Try it.

(Bev kisses her hand; Sheila obeys — half-heartedly.)

BEV: . . . Young birds in the desert have no fear of people . . . They'll come right to you . . . *(She mimes a bird, flapping wings: Lowering her voice.)* And you can kill them . . .

SHEILA: *(Shocked, accusing.)* Did you kill birds?

BEV: No, I passed out. I just remember, all of a sudden, I felt . . . this *chill* . . . a shadow fell on me . . . I thought . . . "Oh, it's a giant bird," but it wasn't . . . It was . . .

SHEILA: *(Cynical.)* Roy.

BEV: It was Roy! He'd walked all that way . . . tracked me . . . There was no one, nothing . . . for miles and miles . . . *(She shivers.)* I don't know if I can tell you this . . . *(Immediately.)* He was naked. We just stared at each other . . . It was a silent thing . . . If we'd spoken, we'd have broken the spell. We met the way men and women met maybe a million years ago . . . silent and for one purpose . . . *(She catches her breath.)* I heard his breathing change . . . Oh, I don't know if I can tell you this . . . It's so strange. At the last second, as much as I wanted him . . . I didn't. When he kissed me, I felt his lips — they were so dry and cracked — the hardest lips I'd ever felt, and I thought, "This isn't a *man,* this is something that's stayed too long in the sun . . . some old Gila monster going to devour me with his poison tongue" . . . His tongue seemed unnaturally long and thick . . . It just kept unraveling . . . *(She demonstrates — Kabuki-style as if unfurling a ribbon from her mouth.)*

SHEILA: Oh, stop!

(Sheila half-jokingly buries her face on the bedding. Bev re-enacts the scene, driving a dazed Sheila backward on the bed. Bev rests, poised, male-style, on her palms at an aggressive angle toward the mesmerized Sheila.)

BEV: He held me down . . . He had me at my wrists. I felt his knee against mine . . . He made me open, and he broke into me, broke into me the way men used to break into women . . . I even heard a little voice at the back of my head say, "He's breaking and entering."

SHEILA: *(Partially rising.)* He forced you!

BEV: No! He wasn't rough . . . He was . . . He was . . . the opposite . . .
(She smiles.) I kept my eyes closed . . . I was afraid to look, afraid of
what I'd see in his face — you know how they can look — *(She imitates routine male huffing and puffing.)* — but he kept on and on . . .
with this . . . this enforced tenderness . . . and finally . . . I wanted
to . . . see him. . . . And there he was, smiling down at me — the
sun behind his head — he had a kind of . . . corona. I could see his
smile, his golden shoulders . . . He was looking right into my eyes,
as if to say: "See. It's all right." And it was all right . . . wasn't it?
*(Bev, stunned by her own account, abruptly backs away from Sheila and
moves to sit a distance from her on the bed.)*

SHEILA: I don't know. It's a bit borderline.

BEV: Oh, I've made it sound all heavy breathing and it wasn't . . . oh, well,
(Amending with a smile.) it *was* . . . But it was more than that . . .
Oh, Sheila, we just *fit* . . . Even his tongue made a kind of sense . . .
(Confidential.) I don't know if I can tell you this . . . *(Instantly.)* He
can make love with his cheeks. . . . Have you ever done this? *(She
imitates a cat-like cheek rub.)*
*(Sheila shakes her head "no" to the cheek-rubbing question. Bev rubs
Sheila's cheek with her own; Sheila backs away.)*

BEV: Don't be scared. You know I'm not that way. It was just some feeling. It didn't come from me. It passed through the room . . . like a
breeze.

BEAUTIFUL BODIES

Laura Shaine Cunningham

This is a comic drama about a gaggle of women friends having a baby shower for one of their number, who is pregnant but unmarried. During the course of the party, the women confront many unpleasant truths about their lives as they examine the choices they have made, resulting in success, to varying degrees, in their careers, at the cost of no husband, no children. In this, the opening scene of the play, Nina is the first arrival to the party, being hosted by Jessie in her NYC loft. Both women are early-to-mid-thirties.

> *The stage is dark. A sudden, single beam of light illuminates the figure of a young woman (Jessie). The momentary vision — a woman, kneeling in profile. Then: darkness. Next: A backdrop of lower Manhattan flickers into view. The effect accelerates as if dusk has fallen on the city and the downtown buildings have begun to light up the night sky. The view is that of a second floor loft in NoHo. We see the sparkle of high rise offices, the giant clock face. The night cityscape is close, dominating. Now, interior lamps begin to illuminate the loft itself. We now see that Jessie is kneeling center-stage in her living room. The loft has been created from a factory space, and throughout, Jessie's warm, beautiful touch does battle with the industrial design. The set should not be strictly "real" but can be stylized: seating platforms instead of sofas, a token Deco floor lamp: artifacts of more gracious times. The loft is not slick, but still raw. Only as Jessie's rose-colored lampshades light do we enter her softer world. We see a kitchen area, stage left, with a meal in progress being cooked. Also stage left: a bathroom door. Downstage right: a freight-style elevator door. The loft has been prepared for an informal gathering: Odd chairs or floor pillows form a semicircle. In the center, an antique bassinet. Jessie kneels to arrange this bassinet, then moves with increased speed to finish her preparations for the party. She drops a hen or two on the floor, rescues them, and wipes them clean. She tries to "hide" cooking mess,*

*stashing pots, shoving trash bag aside. She fusses with the answering ma-
chine, sets her cell phone on the coffee table, then conceals it in a small
purse. She turns on her CD player — a fugue sounds. Instantly, she
switches to something lighter. She runs around, applying last-minute
touches. She pauses, stares at herself in a wall mirror. For an instant,
she is soulful, reflective. She touches her hand to her left breast, sets it
down. Shakes her head, as if to bring herself from reverie into the business at hand. As she places a toy — a baby lamp — in the basket, it
begins to baaaah.*

JESSIE: *(Ironic.)* Jesus.

(She is trying to silence the baah-ing lamp, when the door buzzer shrills.)
JESSIE: *(As she runs to answer the door.)* Who is it?
NINA: *(Offstage.)* Me.

*(Nina enters. Nina is also thirty-three, but is an altogether bigger woman:
bigger voice, bigger breasts. She even wears bigger rings. Nina is tall but
somehow helpless-looking; she tries a touch too hard to be cheery. She
enters, bundled for winter weather, shivery as if she was caught in a bitter wind. As she removes her heavy coat, we see she is faddishly dressed
in a designer outfit that is almost too small. She carries shopping bags
and a cake box. Nina and Jessie kiss, ritually, missing each other's cheeks.
They trade pleasantries in unison.)*

JESSIE & NINA: You look terrific. *(They inspect one another.)* I mean it. You
look terrific.

JESSIE: You've done something. Your hair. Your hair was never red.
NINA: It oxidized.
JESSIE: It suits you. It is you. *You* look great.
NINA: And you? Are you *pink?* You have the look. Did you meet some-
one?

JESSIE: I'm not talking. *(She beams.)*
NINA: You don't have to say a word! *(She grabs her and dances a little.)* Oh,
I'm so happy for you! You've got to tell me. So who is he? He was
obviously wonderful . . . Someone you met on assignment?

JESSIE: I'm not talking. You look great!
NINA: Oh, I can't stand it when you're discreet. I tell you everything and
you never talk! *(A breath.)* A bum molested me on my way over . . .

JESSIE: Really? No one molests *me* anymore . . . *(Suspicious.)* Was he wearing a military greatcoat, and a hat with earflaps? And his pants kind of . . . hanging down unzipped . . . ?

NINA: Yes.

JESSIE: Oh, I know the one. He's always on this block. I don't know how he can expose himself in this cold . . .

NINA: Last part of a man's body to freeze. He waved it at me, Jessie: Does that count as molestation? He didn't touch me . . . He just made noises . . . *(She imitates lip-smacking, kissing sounds.)*

JESSIE: He used to do that when I walked by. Now, he offers me drugs. *(She sighs.)* "Ecstasy." Until recently, I found him . . . disgusting. Now, I feel sorry for him — tugging himself in below-zero weather, yanking away for what . . . some carnal consolation? To forget some old injury, some psychic pain?

NINA: Boo Hoo. Save your sympathy for me. *(Handing her the cake box.)* Here. It's a flourless collapsed chocolate soufflé cake with a fondant center.

JESSIE: Oh, a chocolate cake!

NINA: Don't let me eat any of it. I baked it but I won't eat it. It's for all of you. *(Pause.)* I'll just watch. *(Pause.)* I can't eat till Thursday. *(She waves a Diet Center packet.)* I'll just mix up my little packet when you all eat. I haven't had solid food since I had a Hebrew National kosher frank with everything on the Fourth of July.

JESSIE: No! You have to eat! I've stuffed five Cornish hens. *(She gestures toward kitchen.)* It looks like a Cornish hen mass murder in there.

NINA: It's okay. . . . I still take pleasure in watching others eat. It's become a kind of spectator sport for me.

(Jessie's cell phone beeps in her purse. Jessie startles. Grabs the purse, drops the phone, strains to hear.)

JESSIE: Hello? Hello? I can't hear you . . . *(She sets cell phone back in her purse.)*

JESSIE: Static. Sounds like an attack on Mars. Damn thing. I swore I'd never get one, and now I have. It's always beeping. . . . For a second, I thought my purse was talking to me, the voice of materialism speaking up for itself.

NINA: You jumped on that phone like your life depended on it.

(Jessie stares: maybe her life does depend on it.)

JESSIE: Don't be ridiculous.

NINA: You're expecting him to call?

JESSIE: I wait for no man!

NINA: Yeah. Check your e-mail? That's what I love about today . . . There are so many more ways for a man not to get in touch . . . *(She squints.)* from across The Post Coital Divide. Funny, huh, how a man mates, and then cannot dial your number . . . So what time did he say he'd call? Has he called since you came back to New York? Après sex, across the country — that's another zone. There should be a special calling plan. *To make him call.* I would pay extra for that . . . Friends and Families . . . and Lapsed Lovers . . . So come on, when did he say he would call?

JESSIE: I'm not talking. *(Weakening.)* Not for another hour. And he's out West, so maybe, it will be even later . . .

NINA: Rocky Mountain Time. OH . . . woo*wee*. A cowboy!

JESSIE: Actually, an Indian.

NINA: Oh, my god. I love Indians! With the bone breastplates and the loin cloth?!

JESSIE: Don't be ridiculous. He's a civil liberties lawyer. He wears normal clothes.

NINA: Oh, oh, oh, Dancing with wolves! Come on, tell. I told you about the man in Miami!

JESSIE: I'm not talking. Come on, help me get ready . . . They'll be here in a minute . . . I'm going crazy; I thought I would have more time . . . I had to go to the grocery and the liquor store from the airport . . . I barely got here . . . to set this up . . .

(Nina circles the bassinet, inspects baby shower decorations, preparations.)

NINA: God, Jessie. You don't kid around.

JESSIE: I want Claire to have the whole thing!

(Nina sets her gift boxes on the table. She looks askance at the display.)

NINA: Am I going to have to "ooh" and "aah"?

JESSIE: Over every little bootie.

NINA: Omigod. You'll have to help me. I don't know if I can get through this. I haven't been to a baby shower since the Bronx . . .

JESSIE: They had a lot of them?

NINA: Are you kidding? That's what the boroughs are *for* . . . The boroughs, the suburbs, "the Island," Jersey . . . They're reproduction zones. God, it's fertile out there . . . Everybody reproducing. Half my high school *had* to get married. We didn't use birth control. We just denied sex took place. *(Pause.)* Cynthia Greenspan didn't even make it to graduation. Her water broke in Social Studies. *(Pause.)* Christ. Her kid must be fifteen. I could go out with him. *(She shivers.)* Almost. *(She moves away from the table.)* So who else is coming?

JESSIE: The usuals. Lisbeth. Sue Carol. Martha. Martha might be late. She had a closing uptown. And Claire of course.

NINA: I guess we had to invite Martha.

JESSIE: She would have been hurt.

NINA: She'll ruin everything . . .

JESSIE: No! I planned it perfectly. . . . Martha's coming, but she can't stay . . .

NINA: Martha can always *stay* . . .

JESSIE: *(Laughing self-congratulation.)* Un-unh. Not tonight. It's Donald's birthday. Martha's taking him to dinner at Vert . . . She's had the reservation for eleven months! She has to leave here by eight forty-five, or she'll lose it! *(Exalted.)* So if Claire's late, they may miss each other completely!

NINA: *(Impressed.)* God, you're some hostess. You're sure . . . she can't stay?

JESSIE: That's why I picked tonight. To avoid a disaster. *(Amending.)* Oh, I feel guilty talking about Martha . . .

NINA & JESSIE: *(Ritually, with humor.)* She's basically a good person. *(They laugh.)*

JESSIE: Here . . . have some wine before everyone gets here. Why don't you sit down?

NINA: I look thinner standing up.

JESSIE: Are you okay?

NINA: You want the truth or something we can both live with?

JESSIE: Nina! *(Low voice.)* How's your mother?

NINA: The same. *(Moving away from the tragic topic.)* It's not my mother. They say she's stable.

JESSIE: What then? Something's happened.

NINA: Oh, it's nothing. I saw a guy this afternoon. You know the guy in my mother's building? He's a Zen Buddhist but he's Jewish. He's invited me in for herbal tea a couple of times.

JESSIE: *(Knowing, dry.)* One of the Celestial Seasonings guys.

NINA: "Red Zinger." I thought maybe he was some kind of monk. Or asexual. I put him in the "friend" category. You know — "nothing doing." Then, Sunday, I ran into him in the laundry room, and he said out of the blue — he had had a vision. He's been celibate for five years . . . so I thought — "I better *go* for it!"

JESSIE: He sounds like a good possibility.

NINA: Oh, he's unique! He had it all planned. We had to fast for three days first — that was easy for me — I was almost *there*. . . . then I could come to him — today — dressed only in pure non-synthetic fibers, and we'd be able to do it. . . . It was such a cuckoo offer, I said "yes." So I went up there . . .

JESSIE: What happened?

NINA: Don't ask, and I won't tell you . . .

BINGO BABES
Isabel Duarte

Mary and Peggy are friends, both in their early forties, both heavy smokers. They are in a bingo hall waiting for the bingo to start. This is the opening scene of the play.

> *Mid-morning. It's a smoky, very noisy bingo hall. Mary and Peggy sit at a table, with cards, snacks, and various "good-luck" items on the table in front of them (including photos, dabbers, stuffed animals, and Peggy's small Buddha figure). Both women are smoking. Mary is hooked up to an oxygen tank.*

MARY: If he really cared about you, he'd think, "She's gotta be with Mary. Where else would she go? Mary's the best friend she's got in the whole world. Hey, I happen to know where she lives, and where she hangs out, so that's where I'm goin'. I'm goin' to get me my woman back."

PEGGY: You think so?

MARY: It's as clear as day. Anyone can see that.

PEGGY: Maybe he hasn't noticed I've left. He'd been drinkin'. Don't forget about that.

MARY: You've been gone an entire morning, and he hasn't noticed you're gone? Sure he's noticed. Means he can get on fine without you. Always told you he was a bad appreciator.

PEGGY: What if he really drank too much even for him, and what if he's still passed out, and then he throws up, and chokes to death?

MARY: Only time will tell.

PEGGY: It might be too late.

MARY: Go on and see that he's OK then.

PEGGY: *(Rising.)* Yeah, maybe I should.

MARY: Don't forget your tail.

PEGGY: *(Beat.)* It'll be all my fault. I'm the one who looks after him.

MARY: When are you going to think about you for a change? The game's gonna start any minute.

PEGGY: But I can't be having fun when I think he might be dead, or about to die.

MARY: He's in la-la land.

PEGGY: How would you know?

MARY: 'Cause he's always passed out.

PEGGY: What if I'm gone all day, and then I'll be too nervous to go home for the night, so I'll stay with you. And then when he doesn't show up for his shift, somebody comes over and finds his body? And when we wake up, it's all over the papers and the TV and then in a day or two the police put two and two together and I'll be the one everyone is lookin' for because the whole city'll know that it's 'cause of me that he's dead.

MARY: Go on, then, save the man who don't give a toot for you or your feelings.

PEGGY: He cares about my feelings.

MARY: Um-huh?

PEGGY: Sometimes, sure.

MARY: Sure.

PEGGY: Or at least even if he's not caring about my feelings, at least he's caring about me.

MARY: Oh, I can see how you might think that.

PEGGY: Yeah.

MARY: If you're stupid!

PEGGY: *(Stuttering.)* Wh- What are you telling me?

MARY: What you heard me tell you.

PEGGY: What? That you don't think he loves me?

MARY: Course he does. *(Beat.)* In his own way, that is, yeah, he might love you. Unfortunately, that way ain't much good to you. He can't help it, it's the way he is. And you deserve a whole lot better, don't you think?

PEGGY: Like what?

MARY: Well, like someone with good morals. A nice personality. A little handsome even. Someone who I can look at and say, "What a good guy for my Peggy." Don't you worry. When I spot a good one for ya, I'll know it.

PEGGY: Aren't you going to grab him first?

MARY: No. I ain't ready yet.

PEGGY: By now, shouldn't you —

MARY: Hasn't been long enough. And don't get me started on whose fault that was anyway. *(Beat.)* I just want to play some bingo. Can't you let me do that? As soon as the game starts, I want to feel free from all my worries.

PEGGY: I remember being free. Those were the days, weren't they?

MARY: I don't want to think back no more. I only wanna play.

PEGGY: How did things get like they are?

MARY: Don't make me sad, Peg. Not now.

PEGGY: I wish I could go back for one more day. Even an hour. I'd do everything I could.

MARY: Ah, I knew it, there ya go again.

PEGGY: No, it's more like I'd undo everything I could. Maybe things would be different now.

MARY: Can't be havin' a simple conversation without you sticking your head in the old time machine, trying to see if it'll work, when everyone past the age of five knows you don't move back.

PEGGY: And we'd be in high school, just like how your girls are, and we know all the moves.

(Demonstrating the "walk.")

MARY: It ain't quite like that. *(Demonstrating her version.)* Once you got it, it never leaves you!

PEGGY: We were the coolest girls in the school.

MARY: By the beginning of tenth grade.

PEGGY: At that first dance of the year, everyone is lookin' at us 'cause they know it.

MARY: And they're wonderin' what happened with that cop? We're the reason that they came to school that week, to get the girls who had "destroyed" the pinball machine at the burger hang out.

PEGGY: It was an accident anyways, not that anyone would have believed us.

MARY: So we bullshitted and told him that we didn't do nothin'.

PEGGY: Even before we got any further, Gord was walkin' down the hallway, and he went up to that cop and said he was the one that done it. Said nothing a cop could do scared him anymore, and began slamming himself into lockers and screaming for that cop to stop punching him, that he was sorry about the pinball machine.

MARY: And I'll never forget how he whispered into that cop's face, "You forget that stinkin' pinball machine and I'll forget what you've done." And then he bolted before everyone who had rushed out of their classes reached us.

PEGGY: Imagine that, a sixteen-year-old kid sayin' that to a cop.

MARY: He was a wild one, that boy. Out of control. Handsome as he was fierce.

PEGGY: Nothing could hold him.

MARY: Nor no one either.

PEGGY: He sure was something fine.

MARY: My girls remind me of the best parts of him. There's always something that they do that pulls him to my mind. Every day. Sometimes I wish that it weren't the case, but then, I think, what the hell, it's that way, so now I'm used to it. Then I know it's time to take a break, grab a beer or play some bingo.

PEGGY: Wouldn't you want one more day like that? Wouldn't you want to see your Gord how he was back then, before all the trouble began?

MARY: I don't wanna talk about him no more. The more outta sight he is, the more outta mind. I don't know why I let you take me with you on another one of your memory talks.

PEGGY: I can't help it. It makes me sad too. But I was happy then, when I was a girl. I dunno. Did all this stuff in our life mess us up because that's just what happened and the way things are? Or did we mess it up? On purpose, I mean? Was it us who did this to us, or did someone else plan it and we had no choice?

MARY: How the hell should I know? Besides, it ain't a mess — just a little spill.

PEGGY: I dunno, Mary. It seems like too big mess to clean up. And if we did, how would we? We're too old for high school. And school ain't for everybody.

MARY: No kiddin'. Who needs it? Plenty of people are doing well without it —

PEGGY: You can start a business even. Just look at all the people who come to this country with nothin' except some hope —

MARY: I'm hoping that you'll shut up and let me enjoy my day.

PEGGY: Why didn't we?

MARY: Did you know there's a series of jackpots on for tomorrow?

PEGGY: Why haven't we done well? What did we do wrong?

MARY: It don't look to me like you got enough cards to keep you busy.

PEGGY: Can't you answer me?

MARY: What if we won? My girls are on my case about new clothes for a school dance tomorrow night. Wouldn't that be something?

PEGGY: How come we got nothing?

MARY: I got my girls, and I got my bingo. Everything else, including all your talk, is bullshit!

PEGGY: My feelings are something! And I'm tired of you not paying them any attention. And I got thoughts. And I can't take how I sometimes get, when I wanna scream out, "Hey, I want to start over. Somebody let me take this part of my life over again!"

MARY: When are you going to lighten up?

PEGGY: Maybe when I don't feel this frustrated no more. It ain't right to live like this, without tryin' to do somethin' about it, even if we can do nothing about it. Shouldn't we even be tryin'?

MARY: Well, you done a good thing today. You left before he got up and saved yourself the continuation of that fight with Bag of Bones. You should make it permanent, but that ain't my business. So I ain't saying any more on that subject again. But if ya left him, then things would go back to the old way soon, you'd see.

PEGGY: So many times when I feel like I'm slippin' off this damn earth, that's when Rusty, with a touch of his flesh against mine, or a look deep into the dark cave of my secrets, takes me and puts the bottoms of my feet on the moon, and nothing nor no one can shove me off until I'm good and ready.

MARY: If ya left him, you'd be just terrific. In time, maybe you'll see how right I am, but I won't say anymore.

PEGGY: I hate time 'cause all it does is pull me further away from the best part of my life.

MARY: Stay in the present, would ya? There's more to life than what you're seeing. Being popular in high school wasn't as glamorous as you think. And there's always the one who's better liked than all the others. Don't seem quite fair.

PEGGY: Yeah, you're right. It's no big deal now.

MARY: Who cares?

PEGGY: Yeah, who cares?

MARY: That's a good attitude.

PEGGY: You too! Glad you ain't jealous no more.

MARY: Jealous? Of what?

PEGGY: Ya know. *(Beat.)* Of me.

MARY: Like I said, "Of what?"

PEGGY: You damn well know that I was the most popular one.

MARY: That's a lie. Anyone would tell you that it was me.

PEGGY: Anyone you'd pay. Anyone else would tell you the truth. It was me.

MARY: Anyone you slept with, and granted, that's a lot of teams, but I was still the popular girl. I've known that all these years, so don't you be tryin' to re-do my history.

PEGGY: You have a bad memory.

MARY: Who was the best guy? Gord, right? And who dated Gord? Right. And who even lost their virginity to him —

PEGGY: You too?

MARY: That ain't funny.

PEGGY: Sorry. Come on, it's a joke.

MARY: From now on, no more mention of Gord. The score is 3-0. Bingo! I win.

(Their voices rise as they bicker.)

PEGGY: Wrong. You married him.

MARY: You lousy ex-best friend!

PEGGY: I'm only pointin' out the truth of things.

BLACK THANG
Ato Essandoh

Keisha and Mattie are two women in their twenties, who share an apartment.

Mattie and Keisha's apartment. Miles Davis plays in the background.

KEISHA: Okay. So Adam. Why were you seeing Adam?

MATTIE: He had a motorcycle.

KEISHA: Why'd you stop seeing him?

MATTIE: I joined Greenpeace. Couldn't deal with the motorcycle anymore.

KEISHA: Mm-hmm. And how about Matt? Why were you seeing Matt?

MATTIE: His name was Matt. You know. Mattie. Matt. Get it?

KEISHA: Why'd you stop seeing him?

MATTIE: His name was Matt. You know. Mattie. Matt. Get it?

KEISHA: Thor?

MATTIE: Thor. Always wanted to date a Thor. So I did. One day I asked him if he had a magic hammer. He didn't get it. So I stopped seeing him.

KEISHA: Aha. Apollo?

MATTIE: Same idea as the Thor thing.

KEISHA: What about Dan?

MATTIE: Dan?

KEISHA: Dan . . . Dan . . . Forget it. Alex?

MATTIE: Alex! Loved his cat. Great cat. Love, love, loved that cat.

KEISHA: And why'd you stop seeing him?

MATTIE: The cat died.

KEISHA: Uh-huh. So then what about Sam?

MATTIE: Sam?

KEISHA: Yeah. Why are you seeing Sam?

MATTIE: Um . . . I don't know.

KEISHA: You don't know?

MATTIE: No . . . No . . . I don't know.

KEISHA: *(Makes a gesture indicating how "big" Sam is.)* You don't know?

MATTIE: Oh stop it Keisha. I hate when you do shit like that.

KEISHA: Oh please Mattie. It's not like this is anything new. You guys all want black men. And it's not like they don't want you. Mm-hmm. I mean look at all these famous athletes and actors and politicians all got some fake-tittied, fake-tanned, fake-collagen-lipped, chippy-cha white chick in the stands rooting for them — talking about how they love these women because they was there since the beginning — completely forgetting about the poor black woman who actually *was* with them back in the day when these tired-ass, shit-talking, forty-drinking, no-job-having niggas wasn't about shit.

(Slight pause.)

MATTIE: What are you talking about?

KEISHA: Huh? Nothing. Oh come on Mattie I was just playing. It's just that you always have some trifling reason to sleep with someone. So he's black. Whatever. I mean come on, you just admitted to sleeping with someone because you liked his cat.

MATTIE: You didn't know that cat. You never knew that cat!

KEISHA: Mattie. Why are you so afraid to dig deeper into the emotional core of your relationships —

MATTIE: Keisha. I am not doing the Oprah thing with you right now —

KEISHA: I mean look at Omar and I. Don't you want that?

MATTIE: What you and Omar have? I don't think so.

KEISHA: What's that supposed to mean?

MATTIE: Well it's just that Omar's never really around and you guys are engaged —

KEISHA: He's busy. He works hard. He has a job. He works hard okay? —

MATTIE: I know but —

KEISHA: He works very hard —

MATTIE: I know. I just . . . Look I didn't mean anything by it. Okay?

KEISHA: Mm-hmm.

MATTIE: Keisha.

KEISHA: What?

MATTIE: Nothing.

(Pause.)

KEISHA: *(Indicating music.)* This is nice.

MATTIE: Yeah. It's Miles Davis. Sam let me borrow it. It's like a really rare bootleg or something. It's really nice isn't it?

KEISHA: Yeah. Too bad you'll have to give it back when you dump him.

BOYS AND GIRLS
Tom Donaghy

This play is a delightfully offbeat comedy about same-sex parenting. Bev and Shelly (thirties) are a couple who want to have a father for their baby. They have asked a gay male friend if he will oblige.

> *Reed looks toward Bev and Shelly's apartment, where Shelly finds Bev finishing a phone call.*

SHELLY: Okay, let's not get excited.

BEV: I'm fine.

SHELLY: Don't get all excited.

BEV: You're the one who's up.

SHELLY: What did he say?

BEV: He said —

SHELLY: No, verbatim, the words.

BEV: Yes.

SHELLY: What exactly did he say? You were on the phone. Where was he?

BEV: On the phone.

SHELLY: No, calling from.

BEV: I don't know.

SHELLY: You don't know where he was calling from?

BEV: He was —

SHELLY: Come on.

BEV: He was calling from the other end of the line!

SHELLY: Okay, he was home probably and he said what?

BEV: He said yes.

SHELLY: Verbatim — yes, a firm yes?

BEV: A yes to —

SHELLY: And this was what time?

BEV: — to proceeding. He had questions. This was just before you came in.

SHELLY: And that's when? That's when?

BEV: You came in right in the middle. What — ?

SHELLY: When was that?

BEV: You came in! It was ten minutes ago.

SHELLY: Bev! Exactly?

BEV: I guess!

SHELLY: Good, so he must've been home. Good.

BEV: Yes.

SHELLY: He was in a place where decisions — surrounded by things, books, his things that remind him — pictures, family photos — of his life. Friends, vacations, in a good place, so this doesn't sound —

BEV: He was fine.

SHELLY: — capricious —

BEV: He was having a drink.

SHELLY: — or jumped — to. A drink of what?

BEV: Lemonade.

SHELLY: He said that?

BEV: Strychnine, I don't know. He said he'd taken the phone to the roof and it was hot —

SHELLY: On the roof?

BEV: — so he'd brought up something —

SHELLY: On the roof?

BEV: He's got that little deck thing.

SHELLY: I've never been there.

BEV: I could hear ice — and he said it was hot there.

SHELLY: What, a cocktail?

BEV: Oh, for Christ —

SHELLY: On the fucking roof?

BEV: I'm not going to have this conversation.

SHELLY: You heard ice in a glass on the roof?

BEV: Please, it was lemonade! It wasn't a "drink."

SHELLY: People put booze in lemonade.

BEV: He'd squeezed some —

SHELLY: They put vodka in, it's allowed!

BEV: It was a fucking power drink or something! He's working out — some fruit drink! There wasn't booze in it! It's 9 A.M. for Chrissake!

SHELLY: That hasn't stopped him in the past!

BEV: Please.

SHELLY: Or you.

BEV: Here we go.

SHELLY: Him or you. In the past. If it was the morning — why not? The sun never stopped either of you! The sun in the morning never got in the way of anyone's cocktails in that group!

BEV: I'm not going to proceed if you're going to be all cunty. Do me the courtesy, please, of not being totally cunty. Please. You just turn into this raving, paranoid, twelve-foot cunt.

SHELLY: Forget the whole thing.

BEV: And two isn't a group.

SHELLY: What, please?

BEV: You called us a group.

SHELLY: Whatever.

BEV: Two isn't a group.

SHELLY: Well, it's something.

BEV: It certainly is.

SHELLY: Forget the whole thing.

BEV: He's coming over.

SHELLY: When? To talk to me?

BEV: You're half the battle.

SHELLY: That's good.

BEV: Tonight.

SHELLY: That's good.

BEV: Okay.

SHELLY: I'll smell his breath, for one. *(Beat.)* But good. Shows he's serious.

BEV: You're not going to smell his breath.

SHELLY: Shows he understands the seriousness. He wouldn't dare come over drunk. *(Beat.)* I know it was the past and I'm sorry.

BEV: He's changed for fuck's sake.

SHELLY: I know.

BEV: I've changed. I had to. And I did. Less — less — less — you know — more — more adult. I had to! I would have sooner or later. But I was impelled. Our relationship. What was being offered —

SHELLY: You know I'm grateful.

BEV: — what could be exponentially —

SHELLY: I am —

BEV: — more.

SHELLY: — and you don't know.

BEV: More all around.

SHELLY: You don't know. How grateful. I get up every morning and look at you asleep and think — ! You don't know I know. The faith you've had.

BEV: Thank you.

SHELLY: And I know.

BEV: *(Beat.)* He was good to me. Before you. Before you there was someone who was good to me, in his way. That should — and we shouldn't be threatened by those who loved our lovers before us. We should be — please — grateful.

SHELLY: When did you say he was coming?

BEV: He just said tonight.

SHELLY: Do we have anything in the fridge?

BEV: I said we'd got out for dinner.

SHELLY: Did we finish the pears?

BEV: No, we bought too many.

SHELLY: They're just going to rot if we don't eat them.

BEV: Let 'em rot!

SHELLY: *(Beat.)* And he said dinner?

BEV: I said we would pick a place and call so he could dress appropriately.

SHELLY: And where's Georgie?

BEV: On his play date.

SHELLY: Good. And when does the play date end?

BEV: It's open-ended until they get cranky.

(They reach for each other's hands.)

SHELLY: Good.

BEV: Thank you.

SHELLY: Can we make love? It's been weeks.

BEV: Shell, everything we're doing —

SHELLY: I miss you.

BEV: I'm right here. I'm tired.

SHELLY: You sure? *(Beat.)* Okay.

BEV: We will.

SHELLY: Call him and tell him eight.

BEV: Can I call in a bit? I need to take a walk.

BUFFALO GIRL
A. R. Gurney

Amanda, a former TV star who has fallen on hard times, has returned to her hometown of Buffalo, New York, where she is playing Madame Ranevskaya in *The Cherry Orchard*. Here, she is talking to Jackie, the director. Amanda is probably in her fifties; Jackie in her thirties.

JACKIE: *(Settling in.)* Now for the tough stuff.

AMANDA: I thought my agent did all that.

JACKIE: He hasn't been very communicative lately.

AMANDA: He doesn't want me to do this.

JACKIE: No kidding.

AMANDA: It's strictly a money thing. He thinks I should do more television.

JACKIE: Do you want to?

AMANDA: It's so tiring, television. You throw yourself into it, you reach out, but nothing comes back. It's like talking on the telephone when someone may have hung up. I need to reconnect.

JACKIE: You're hungry for an audience.

AMANDA: Starved!

JACKIE: One thing about this theater, we're developing a good one. *(Handing her a sheet of paper.)* Here's your bio, by the way. For the program.

AMANDA: Didn't they send you a press kit?

JACKIE: We want to emphasize the Buffalo thing.

AMANDA: *(Putting on her glasses, reading the bio.)* May I have a pencil, please?

JACKIE: *(Handing her one.)* Here.

AMANDA: *(Crossing things out.)* No . . . No . . . and no.

JACKIE: What's wrong?

AMANDA: No dates, please. I was born and went to school here. Period . . . And no on the private school. That makes people think I'm a shallow Wasp with a drinking problem, which of course I am . . . And don't say I "immediately" won a Critic's Circle Award when I went to New York.

JACKIE: You didn't?

AMANDA: Not by a long shot. I spent three years doing repertory, working with the best. We did Shakespeare and Strindberg and Molière. They were planning to give me Ibsen's Nora when Hollywood nabbed me.

JACKIE: *(Taking back the bio; making notes.)* . . . Where you went on to win . . . *(Checks her notes.)* Two Academy Award nominations.

AMANDA: Eventually. Down the line. For supporting player . . .

JACKIE: And three Emmys.

AMANDA: Haven't done much of anything lately.

JACKIE: You were on the tube the other night.

AMANDA: Playing a judge. Everybody does that when they need money. Which I do. But don't say that either.

JACKIE: Of course not.

AMANDA: I'm broke, frankly. *(Indicating her script.)* Like Madame Ranevskaya. I never could save much out there, what with the house in Hollywood Hills and the inevitable shrink. And you probably read somewhere how one of the men I married walked off with all my savings. And — did I mention my daughter?

JACKIE: You did.

AMANDA: She's in and out of institutions.

JACKIE: I didn't know that.

AMANDA: Manic-depressive. Lately they say bipolar issues. Sometimes I think she's just plain nuts.

JACKIE: I'm sorry.

AMANDA: Any way you slice it, she's expensive.

JACKIE: I can imagine.

AMANDA: Which is another reason why I took this job.

JACKIE: For the money? Get serious.

AMANDA: A play could get me going again. It happened with Kate Hepburn and Angela Lansbury. They came back and did plays, and went on to write their own ticket.

JACKIE: True enough.

AMANDA: So I've been thinking about that. And about how I need . . .

(Stamps her foot on the stage again.) . . . this again. *(Reaches out toward the auditorium.)* And them, God love them! So when you called and said, "Come home. And do a play *about* coming home," that was it. And it can lead to bigger things down the line.

JACKIE: For all of us.

AMANDA: And I might be able to do something about my daughter. And my grandson.

JACKIE: Grandson?

AMANDA: During one of her mood swings, my daughter managed to deposit on my doorstep an adorable little boy. Along with a nanny who is introducing him to the lilting linguistics of rural Peru.

JACKIE: I didn't know you were a grandmother.

AMANDA: I am, and if you mention that in my bio, I'll throttle you with my bare hands.

JACKIE: OK, OK.

AMANDA: I do not do grandmothers, Jackie. Mothers, yes. Grandmothers, no way. Which is what I told my agent. When I said I was considering a play, he frantically put me up for a stupid sitcom at Fox. Recurring role, minimum pay — three Emmys notwithstanding. A character named Granny Sweetpants. Can you believe it? They even stole the name from L'il Abner.

JACKIE: Sounds grim.

AMANDA: They made me read for the thing.

JACKIE: You auditioned?

AMANDA: I have sunk to that. I met the writers — a couple of kids just out of kindergarten. They wanted me to wear a gray fright wig and come into a suburban kitchen, and make jokes about Viagra. I said Thanks but no thanks. I am returning to the stage. I'm playing Madame Lubov Ranevskaya in *The Cherry Orchard* at a distinguished regional theatah.

JACKIE: You didn't say Buffalo.

AMANDA: People laugh when you say Buffalo.

JACKIE: I want to change that, goddammit.

AMANDA: Anyway, that's why I came back. *(Acts.)* "To my nursery! My own sweet, wonderful room! I slept here as a child . . . And here I am, like a child again."

GOLDEN LADDER
Donna Spector

Catherine and Mary are two teenaged girls. Catherine is dating a Jewish boy named Aaron. Mary offers her some advice.

MARY: *(Enters.)* How come I never see you with Aaron anymore?

CATHERINE: I don't know. He won't talk to me.

MARY: How come?

CATHERINE: He's just being weird.

MARY: Did he want you to go all the way and you said no?

CATHERINE: Something like that.

MARY: I told you Jewish boys have more hormones, y'know, but you wouldn't listen to me.

CATHERINE: I guess you're right.

MARY: So, wanna go over to the high school and watch football practice?

CATHERINE: I guess not.

MARY: The guys look really good in their shorts.

CATHERINE: I'll go some other time.

MARY: All those tan muscles.

CATHERINE: They look dumb running around in their shorts, shoving each other and kicking balls.

MARY: Hunh. *(Beat.)* Are you missing Aaron?

CATHERINE: No. *(Beat.)* Yes.

MARY: Well, look, Cathy, maybe you should just go all the way with him.

CATHERINE: I can't.

MARY: Why not? Then you can tell me what it's like. I hear you *move.*

CATHERINE: What do you mean?

MARY: The boy puts his thing inside the girl and they move around.

CATHERINE: I don't care.

MARY: I think it's weird. I mean, like do they move up and down or around the room?

CATHERINE: Don't talk about it.

MARY: So if you'd just do it with Aaron, we'd know for sure.

CATHERINE: I can't do it with Aaron, stupid! Not if he won't talk to me, and he looks the other way when I pass him in the hall, and yesterday he ate lunch with Francine Shacklin, and they were laughing, and . . . *(She starts to cry.)* I hate him!

MARY: I'm sorry, Cathy. I wish you wouldn't call me stupid though.

CATHERINE: I didn't mean to, but don't talk about Aaron ever again, ever, okay? When I see him in the hall, I'm going to look the other way too, because I don't even want to know he *exists*, okay? And if he goes all the way with Francine Shacklin, I hope he dies!

MARY: Yeah, because she's got all those hormones.

CATHERINE: Oh, shut up!

MARY: What did I say? I didn't mention you-know-who's name.

CATHERINE: Jewish hormones. You're really something, Mary.

MARY: I read it in *Seventeen.*

CATHERINE: *Seventeen.* The ultimate scientific and medical authority.

MARY: I'm going over to the high school now.

CATHERINE: Oh, do. Go watch the dumb boys do push-ups in the mud.

MARY: I don't like you any more.

CATHERINE: Who cares? *(To audience, as Mary exits.)* I didn't like myself either. As Aaron walked through the halls holding hands with Francine Shacklin, waited for her after classes, took her to dances, I'd roll my eyes and make anti-Semitic remarks like, "Oh, those Jews." I became the perfect WASP. *(She addresses an unseen church group.)* As president of the Presbyterian youth group, I want to talk to you about predestination and the damnation of unbelievers. As you know, we are all in the hands of God, who decides who is going to be saved and who, y'know, will be sent to Hell. Now, even though God has already made His decision and there isn't much we can do about it, I mean, actually, not *anything* we can do about it, we still try to be good and follow Jesus' teachings, because we *know* — I mean, it's only *logical* — that God isn't going to save anyone who isn't a Christian, y'know, preferably a *Presbyterian.* And although I do feel sorry for the unbelievers who are going to run in the flames of Hell, it is their decision, isn't it?

SORROWS AND REJOICINGS
Athol Fugard

Both women are in their forties. Marta is a black South African woman. Allison is white. She has returned to South Africa for the funeral of her husband, David, an exiled poet. Marta was David's housekeeper. She is also the mother of his only child.

ALLISON: Did you ever know how jealous I was of you, Marta?

MARTA: Jealous? Of me?

ALLISON: Yes. From the very first time I saw you, trying to be a servant and David trying to be the master, I knew there was something between the two of you. And then I saw little Rebecca on your back I knew for sure. Poor David! He made it so obvious by deliberately ignoring the child when she was in here with you.

MARTA: I could see you didn't like me. But jealous? Ag, no Allison. You were wasting your time being jealous of me — you with all your education and a white skin. I had nothing to give him . . . except trouble and a daughter who doesn't love him.

ALLISON: No, Marta. You had as much to give him as I ever did . . . and maybe even more. It has taken me a long time to be able to say that, but it's true. Apart from being the woman you are, you are also a part of this world that he loved with such passion. You are this world, Marta, in a way that I could never be, no matter how hard I tried . . . and the truth is I didn't try at all. At the time I refused to see that. I refused to see what bound the two of you together. As far as I was concerned you were right: You did have nothing to give him except an illegitimate child and big trouble if the two of you were ever caught as lovers.

MARTA: So what did he say?

ALLISON: When?

MARTA: When you told him that?

ALLISON: I never did. Just thought it to myself.

MARTA: You never talked about me?

ALLISON: Only as "dear Marta the faithful, loyal and devoted servant and friend of the family." At the time I fooled myself that I was being sensitive to his feelings, but the truth is I was afraid of what I would find if I started probing and tried to challenge your place in his life. *(Pause.)* There's something I've always wanted to ask you. Did he make love to you during those visits when I was here with him?

MARTA: Didn't you ever ask him?

ALLISON: Yes, I did.

MARTA: What did he say?

ALLISON: No. He said no.

MARTA: So why do you ask me?

ALLISON: Because I've never been sure if I could believe him.

MARTA: *(After a pause.)* Not when you were here with him. Do you want to know about the other times?

ALLISON: No.

It wasn't easy for me you know. The situation was so damned complicated. Because let's face it, if everything had been different, if this had been a free country back then, mightn't he have married you? Had I got him, like so many other things in my life, because in addition to all my other splendid virtues, I had a white skin? It's called "liberal guilt." Marta, and I suffered from an overdose of it.

MARTA: *(Shaking her head.)* Haai, Allison! . . . and there I was jealous also, hating you because you had taken him away from me.

ALLISON: *(With a wry little laugh at herself.)* Yes, I also thought I had done that, and to make quite certain of it, I decided in London that we would have a family of our own. We had talked about having children in Johannesburg because we both wanted them, but we both also felt that the situation in the country was too dangerous for us to do anything about it. London was different. We were starting a new life! He had a well-paid teaching post, wonderful prospects for his writing, and best of all you were ten thousand miles away. Thanks to that one-way exit permit and the way things were going in the country it looked as if it was going to be a long time before he would see you and Rebecca again.

(Pause. Marta waits expectantly.)

ALLISON: He got mumps.

MARTA: Pampoentjies?

ALLISON: Yes, that's what he called it. Little pumpkins?

MARTA: Ja. Because of the swellings.

ALLISON: Yes, he certainly had those. At the time we didn't know what the consequences could be — in fact we had a few good laughs at it — his testicles came up as big as cricket balls. Anyway, to cut a long story short that was the end of our hopes for a family. I made the mistake once of suggesting that we should think about adopting a child. He said no, he already had a child of his own . . . waiting for him back "home." So I went back to school — London University for a Ph.D. — and David started drinking.

Oh Marta! . . . what a bloody mess it ended up being. And why? Mumps? Can "little pumpkins" destroy a relationship? A life? Was it me? Or you maybe? Or once again just a case of good old South Africa doing what it does best . . . wrecking everything, because that is what we finally had to face up to — our life together had become a shambles.

U.S. DRAG
Gina Gionfriddo

Allison and Angela, two recent college graduates, are looking for ways to make as much money as possible, as quickly as possible, with as little effort as possible. They are getting ready to go to a party.

Back at their apartment, Angela and Allison primp and prepare for the night ahead.

ALLISON: I don't think that no man is good enough for me.

ANGELA: What?

ALLISON: What Christopher said. I don't think that no man is good enough. If you were a guy, you would be good enough! Why can't I find a boy version of you and you find a boy version of me?

ANGELA: Allison, I love you. But a boy version of you is not what I'm looking for.

ALLISON: I know. You can do better than me. You're together. You're not afraid.

ANGELA: Oh, I'm afraid.

ALLISON: Really? What are you afraid of?

(Pause.)

ANGELA: I'm afraid of winding up an old spinster in a dirty rented room eating tuna from a can because I couldn't make up my mind what to do with my life. What are you afraid of?

ALLISON: Sort of the same as you. Not getting it. Watching it on TV when I'm fifty and knowing I missed it.

ANGELA: But what is it?

ALLISON: I don't know. Comfort. Sort of. I mean, it isn't money — exactly — or fame. Although those would be great.

ANGELA: What is it, then?

(Pause.)

ALLISON: I don't know. I just feel sometimes like . . . like we don't know that many people who are . . . worth knowing. Sometimes I feel like you're the only person I know worth knowing and that's great, but . . . you can't just have one person in your life. That's not, like, safe.

ANGELA: *(Echoing Evan.)* You gotta be safe.

ALLISON: I'm serious.

ANGELA: *(Slightly condescending.)* So it's about knowing cooler people?

ALLISON: It's about mattering! I just keep thinking about this guy I went to junior high with. Jeremy Feldman. He was just this geek, this greasy, pimply geek. But he wrote this book. *The Kid's Guide to Quitting Smoking.* All about how fucking hard it was for him when his parents quit smoking. And it got published and suddenly everybody wanted to be his friend. All of a sudden people looked at him like he mattered. *(Pause.)* I just want to matter. The way they looked at us when we were making copies at the magazine . . . Angela they looked at us like we didn't matter!

ANGELA: So write a book.

ALLISON: I can't write. *(Pause.)* I can't act either and I'm not hot enough to be a model. Chelsea Clinton hangs out with Madonna and she doesn't have a talent. That can happen if, you know, you've got talented people near you, but —

ANGELA: You really think your life would change if you were hanging out with Madonna?

ALLISON: Of course it would.

ANGELA: Yeah, but what's fucked up about that, Allison, is that it's Madonna. I mean, you have no evidence that she's like, a good person or a wise person or . . .

ALLISON: That's what I want, OK. So kill me. You think the same way. You get all bent out of shape every time Naomi Wolf, like, breathes.

ANGELA: I'm smarter than she is.

ALLISON: It's the same thing. You want to matter to people you think are worth mattering to. You're the same as me even if you think you aren't. *(Pause.)*

ANGELA: I read this interview with David Duchovny once . . . He was paraphrasing Barthes' idea, in *Camera Lucida,* that the reason we think we know famous people is because we spend lots of time with them in our homes — on TV and CDs, in the newspaper. The repetition of the image and the voice inspires the illusion of intimacy. He was just saying how fucked up it is to have tons of people feel like they know you or want to know you.

ALLISON: Well, boo hoo hoo David Duchovny. I mean, Michael J. Fox having Parkinson's . . . obviously it still sucks, but . . . you can't tell me it doesn't help a whole lot to have, like, Oprah and the whole fucking Senate care about you.

ANGELA: Maybe.

ALLISON: I don't want to get Parkinson's and have nobody care.

ANGELA: You're not going to get Parkinson's. But if you did, I would care.

ALLISON: Even if you had, like, a couple kids and some big job?

ANGELA: Of course.

(Pause.)

ALLISON: We should still have more friends.

ANGELA: Just to be safe.

ALLISON: Seriously, we should.

ANGELA: OK, let's go make some.

WHERE'S MY MONEY?
John Patrick Shanley

Two friends (both twenties to thirties) who haven't seen each other in a while are meeting for coffee in a café. Natalie is a no-nonsense business-woman. Celeste has delusions that she is an actress. Celeste is engaged to be married — to a very odd man, who's married to someone else . . .

Lights up on a French coffee café in Soho. We're outside. It's late morn-ing. We see Celeste, a darkly attractive woman with a slightly Bohemian feel, talking on a cell phone. She sits at a little blue table, with a hot drink and the remains of a muffin. There's a notebook and paper on the table as well. She has a low voice. She's excited and alarmed by the call.

CELESTE: Wait! She tied knots in his tie, she shoved the tip up his tushie, and then, at the key moment, she ripped the tie out like she was start-ing a lawn mower. Pup pup pup pup PWONK! The last knot was huge. But here's the twisted part. The next day he goes to the office — wearing the tie. Other than that, it wasn't a very good movie. What? What's that? I can't. I can't! I'm in a public place. Turquoise. You are? Right now? You mean for real? I'd like to see that. *(Natalie appears. She's about the same age, also attractive, a little harder maybe, more pros-perous. She recognizes Celeste and points and waves. Celeste mimes shock and happiness at seeing Natalie. The following big of dialogue is over-lapped in.)* Natalie! *(She gestures she needs a minute more on the phone, and then says into the receiver.)* Can you hold a second? Shut up! *(Cov-ers the receiver.)* Natalie! How are you? Oh my God!

NATALIE: I'm getting coffee. Should I join you? You have a minute?

CELESTE: Yes! I'll finish up while you're . . .

NATALIE: Great! *(Natalie goes in. Celeste resumes her call.)*

CELESTE: I gotta go. What about . . . *(The caller cuts her off.)* What's Fri-day like for you, Friday night? Kenny's got a gig. Okay, I'll be there. That's just my number. Okay. See ya then.

(She puts her cell away. Natalie returns with coffee.)

NATALIE: Hey Celeste, whadaya know? It's so great to see you!

CELESTE: You too!

NATALIE: Where did you go?

CELESTE: Where did YOU go? You dropped out of the world! You look great, Natalie. You look really put together.

NATALIE: I sort've am together.

CELESTE: Did I hear you got married?

NATALIE: Two years.

CELESTE: Congratulations!

NATALIE: Thank you. You look so hokie stokie!

CELESTE: What does that mean?

NATALIE: Sex bomb.

CELESTE: I'll accept that.

NATALIE: Are you still with that guy?

CELESTE: Kenny. Yeah.

NATALIE: In the same place?

CELESTE: Yeah, same place. THE ROOM. Where are you?

NATALIE: Upper West Side. Two rooms. It was Henry's aunt's when she . . .

CELESTE: What are we doing? Let's sit. I'm set up over here.

NATALIE: Good idea. *(They sit.)* Well. Here we are. The accounting department.

CELESTE: I was secretarial.

NATALIE: Is that a ring on your finger?

CELESTE: I guess so.

NATALIE: I mean it looks like an engagement ring . . .

CELESTE: *(Simultaneous.)* An engagement ring.

NATALIE: Well, is it?

CELESTE: That's what Kenny called it.

NATALIE: Well, isn't that what it is then?

CELESTE: He didn't exactly ask me. He just said that's what it was.

NATALIE: A guy says "Here's an engagement ring," it isn't a big leap to . . .

CELESTE: Yeah, but he put it on MY Visa card.

NATALIE: Oh. Well that's . . .

CELESTE: Questionable. Yeah.

NATALIE: Are you still acting?

CELESTE: I take classes, but I haven't gotten much work. I have a great coach, but my agent is . . . I'm not even sure I have an agent. I have to get into that. That's the next thing. There's always a next thing.

NATALIE: But I mean . . . did you . . . ?

CELESTE: Did I what?

NATALIE: You know. Get an operation?

CELESTE: No, I never did. I decided against it.

NATALIE: So you still have the limp.

CELESTE: Yeah, but it's not very noticeable.

NATALIE: It was the first thing I registered about you. Here was this sexy young girl, she wants to be an actress, but she has a limp. Can they fix it?

CELESTE: There's nothing really wrong to fix. It's how I'm made. It's just a slight disproportion between my left and right hip. I guess, at a certain point, I decided to accept myself as I am.

NATALIE: So if you're not making money acting, how do you get by?

CELESTE: I temp. I'm a secretarial temp. Just like I always was.

NATALIE: Did I hurt your feelings?

CELESTE: No.

NATALIE: I'm such a rhinoceros.

CELESTE: It's better.

NATALIE: Think so?

CELESTE: At least you tell the truth.

NATALIE: That's what I think, but maybe I'm just an asshole.

CELESTE: Even if you are an asshole — which you're not — at least you don't compound it by pretending to be sensitive.

NATALIE: I did hurt your feelings.

CELESTE: Well, what do you think?

NATALIE: So I did. I thought I did.

CELESTE: You just about said I'll never get a job because I'm a cripple.

NATALIE: An acting job.

CELESTE: Well, I'm an actress!

NATALIE: But you don't work.

CELESTE: Lots of actresses don't work!

NATALIE: And maybe those girls shouldn't be actresses.

CELESTE: You got a mouth on you, you know that? I forgot this charac-
teristic. The truth teller.

NATALIE: Well, I'm an accountant. Bottom line.

CELESTE: When it suits you.

NATALIE: What's that mean?

CELESTE: Stuff.

NATALIE: Huh?

CELESTE: My white enamel alligator pin.

NATALIE: I don't follow.

CELESTE: You liked it.

NATALIE: What?

CELESTE: When we were working together. I had this white enamel pin.
Of an alligator. You liked it, and you did something.

NATALIE: Are we in the same conversation?

CELESTE: I left my jacket over my chair. When I came back from lunch,
my white enamel alligator pin was gone.

NATALIE: This is back three years ago?

CELESTE: Yeah.

NATALIE: Are you saying three years ago you thought I took a pin off your
jacket while you were at lunch?

CELESTE: It's more like a nagging slight unfounded suspicion I want to
definitely put to rest.

NATALIE: There had to be six people in that office, messengers coming
and going, the coffee cart. Why would you think it was me?

CELESTE: I don't know.

NATALIE: Did I seem guilty?

CELESTE: No.

NATALIE: Then how did you come to think I took your pin?

CELESTE: No good reason.

NATALIE: But then why did you think it?

CELESTE: *(Big confession.)* Because the day before, I took your red beret!

NATALIE: You did?

CELESTE: Yes.

NATALIE: I had a red beret? I guess I did. You took it?

CELESTE: Yes. I've been carrying that confession around for three years.

(As she removes the beret from her purse.) Actually, I've been carrying the beret for three years. Here it is back. I'm sorry.

NATALIE: Why would you take this?

CELESTE: Because I'm insane! And then I tried to justify my bad behavior by deciding you took my pin!

NATALIE: But I didn't take your pin!

CELESTE: I know you didn't take it! I wish you had. Then we'd be even. You can just walk away. I'll understand.

NATALIE: Listen. Let's just say we're even, okay? So you took some raggy beret that didn't belong to you. Forgive yourself. We've all done worse.

CELESTE: Thank you.

NATALIE: No big deal.

CELESTE: I'm such a case.

NATALIE: Forget it.

CELESTE: No. You're a nicer person than me.

NATALIE: No I'm not.

CELESTE: Yes, you are. I wanna learn from you. I wanna learn to deal. Maybe I should look at my life without makeup. My life is bad. Well, it's not that bad but . . . I enjoy reading. I don't wanna feel sorry for myself but . . .

NATALIE: Is it Kenny?

CELESTE: He's not helping. But it's him too. I'm not getting work and I'm turning thirty, and I just got this huge bill for the ring . . .

NATALIE: I would've thought you'd already turned thirty?

CELESTE: ALL RIGHT, I've TURNED thirty! So your marriage is good?

NATALIE: I mean, actually, you must be thirty-one.

CELESTE: Yes. All right. I forgot. You ARE an accountant. Thirty-one. I'm glad we got that straightened out. So how's your marriage? Good? Better? Bad?

NATALIE: It's good.

CELESTE: Nice for you. I'm glad. And you have a job you like?

NATALIE: It's solid.

CELESTE: So you see what you're saying? Look at the picture. You've got a life.

NATALIE: Well, I made choices.

CELESTE: *(She cries.)* No. It's karma. I try to make choices, but nothing
sticks. I just float.

NATALIE: How's Kenny doing?

CELESTE: I think Kenny hates me.

NATALIE: He does not!

CELESTE: We've been together for so long, and his life is so not happening, and he is smoking so much dope.

NATALIE: How's the band?

CELESTE: The band broke up. Kenny does weddings now as a pickup deal.
But mostly he just sits in the apartment and looks at me like I'm
"The Thing That Ate His Life."

NATALIE: Is he depressed?

CELESTE: He's a lazy, stoned drummer in a cheap Hawaiian shirt. He's like
a depressing piece of furniture. What's your husband do?

NATALIE: He's a lawyer.

CELESTE: A lawyer. What happened to that other guy?

NATALIE: Who?

CELESTE: You know who.

NATALIE: Tommy. Well, I knew that wasn't going to work out. That was
just sex.

CELESTE: You were nuts about him.

NATALIE: He was a porter. I wasn't going to marry a porter.

CELESTE: Did he ask you?

NATALIE: No.

CELESTE: That was hot. That thing you had with him.

NATALIE: You never saw us.

CELESTE: I remember the way you looked. He was all over the way you
looked.

NATALIE: Yeah, well, it was hot.

CELESTE: I feel like running something by you.

NATALIE: What?

CELESTE: Maybe not.

NATALIE: All right.

CELESTE: I'm having an affair.

NATALIE: Oh wow. Who?

CELESTE: Six months now.

NATALIE: Does Kenny know?

CELESTE: He acts like he doesn't but, I mean . . . There's evidence.

NATALIE: Phone calls?

CELESTE: No. Bruises.

NATALIE: So this guy's violent?

CELESTE: WE'RE violent. We both have a lot of anger. It's sort've Latin.

NATALIE: He's Latin?

CELESTE: No.

NATALIE: Uh-huh. So you hit him, too?

CELESTE: No. But we're in it together. It must sound bad. It's hard to explain.

NATALIE: Why'd you tell me?

CELESTE: I haven't told anybody.

NATALIE: Then why me?

CELESTE: He slaps me. He spanks me. He makes me crawl around the floor like a dog. He calls me names. And then I go home to Kenny and act like nothing happened.

NATALIE: So Kenny knows.

CELESTE: I don't know. Kenny blows so much weed he may think I'm something on TV.

NATALIE: He must know.

CELESTE: Who knows what Kenny knows? He's English.

NATALIE: And this guy you're having this . . .

CELESTE: He has read the book that God wrote on my flesh. I've always been afraid to say what I want. He knows what I want and he makes me do it. Get this. He gave me a gun.

NATALIE: He what?

CELESTE: Sometimes I'd be headed home late. He was worried about me. So he gave me a little gun. How sexy is that? I know. Sick.

NATALIE: Not necessarily. But what's the deal exactly?

CELESTE: There is no deal. I see him about once every week and a half. He calls me, I show up somewhere, and he burns down my fucking house.

NATALIE: He's married.

CELESTE: Yeah. I don't care.

NATALIE: You care.

CELESTE: You know what I mean.

NATALIE: And you know what I mean.

Scenes for
Two Men

MONTHS ON END
Craig Pospisil

This scene takes place in Ben's living room. Walter comes over to console Ben, as he just learned that Ben's fiancée, Phoebe, has dumped him. Both men are in their early thirties.

OCTOBER

A living room. Ben searches for something under the couch. The doorbell rings, and Ben gets up and opens the door. Walter enters.

WALTER: Ben, are you okay?

BEN: Oh, I'm glad you're here. Walter.

WALTER: Elaine just called me. She says Phoebe's at her place crying . . . saying she left you.

BEN: Can you help me with something?

WALTER: Yeah, of course.

BEN: Go into the other room and look under the bed. Tell me if you see anything. *(Ben searches the couch's cushions. Walter is confused, but hurries offstage to the bedroom.)*

WALTER: *(Offstage.)* Ah . . . I had no idea things between you two were bad.

BEN: That's just it. Things have been great. This came out of nowhere. I mean, we're having a little fight . . . and the next thing I know she's packing her bags and she's out the door. *(Slight pause.)* Do you see anything? *(Walter returns.)*

WALTER: No, just dust. *(Slight pause.)* So . . . what did you argue about?

BEN: It's silly when you look at it. *(Slight pause.)* We fought about the Beatles.

WALTER: *(Pause.)* John, Paul, George, and Ringo?

BEN: Yeah. She says I'm too obsessed with the Beatles.

WALTER: What?

BEN: Yeah, can you believe that?

WALTER: What do you mean by obsessed?

BEN: Thank you! That's what I said.

WALTER: No . . . how did the fight start?

BEN: She broke my Yellow Submarine.

WALTER: Yeah, so? Buy a new CD.

BEN: No, not the album. My Yellow Submarine. The Corgi die-cast metal toy manufactured in 1968 and released with the animated movie.

WALTER: Oh, right. A friend of mine had one of those when I was a kid. So . . . Phoebe broke it?

BEN: She was vacuuming and knocked it off its shelf. I came home and found it on the floor with some paint chipped off.

WALTER: *(Pause.)* Is that all?

BEN: All?! No, that's not all! John and Paul fell out of the sub, and . . . and I think she vacuumed them up! She'd already thrown out the garbage, so I ran down to the street, but the trash had been picked up. I've been looking all over the apartment, just in case . . . but nothing.

WALTER: *(Slight pause.)* What fell out?

BEN: John and Paul! There's a button on the side, and when you press it a hatch opens and —

WALTER: John and Paul pop out.

BEN: Right. So, I mean I guess I kind of lost my temper and said, "How could you do that? You've got to be more careful around my Beat-les case."

WALTER: Ben, it was just an accident.

BEN: I know, I know. You should have heard her. "I'm sorry. But you don't have to make me feel so bad. Sometimes I think you care more about your stupid Beatles than me."

WALTER: And what did you say?

BEN: "Are you calling the people who created *Sgt. Pepper's Lonely Hearts Club Band* stupid?! Are you insane?!"

WALTER: How could you say that?

BEN: She lost John and Paul!

WALTER: It's just a toy!

BEN: Toy, hell. I paid four hundred dollars for that submarine. Now it's chipped and John and Paul are gone. That drops the price to a hundred and fifty dollars at most.

WALTER: Are you kidding me?

BEN: Who'd want a Yellow Submarine without John and Paul?

WALTER: You paid four hundred dollars for an old toy?

BEN: It's a collector's item.

WALTER: Who pays that much for a toy that isn't two hundred years old?

BEN: Beatles collectors.

WALTER: *(Pause.)* All right, leaving that aside for a moment . . . she says, you care for the Beatles more than her. You call her crazy . . . and then what happened?

BEN: She ran out of the room crying.

WALTER: Please tell me you went after her.

BEN: Well, I . . . I wanted to. But . . . I had to go downstairs to check the garbage.

WALTER: Oh, yes. Of course.

BEN: But when I got back up here and saw she was packing, I got very emotional, really upset.

WALTER: All right, good. I hope you told her you were sorry.

BEN: Yeah, of course. I apologized over and over. And I said, "Please don't go. Today of all days."

WALTER: Uh-huh, and . . . "Today of all days"?

BEN: It's October ninth. John Lennon's birthday. I always like to light a candle, have some wine, and listen to *Abbey Road* or something. She knows what that means to me.

WALTER: Every year?

BEN: Yeah, and this year's special because I just took all my Beatles collectible out of storage.

WALTER: Yeah, I noticed. There's Beatles' stuff all over your bedroom.

BEN: Well, I decided, this is part of who I am, you know. And what's the point in having these things if they're not out where you can enjoy them?

BEN: But do you really need two display cases of . . . I don't know what.

WALTER: Aren't those great? They're arranged chronologically, so the first case has memorabilia from 1960 to '65. There's Beatle bubble bath and beach towels, hair cream, tour programs, even panty hose. Then the second case goes from '66 to 1970, so it's got a lot of Yellow Submarine stuff, like puzzles and stationery. I've even got two lunch boxes. With no rust on them at all.

WALTER: *(Slight pause.)* Ben . . . have you been drinking?

BEN: What? No!

WALTER: Well, Phoebe's right.

BEN: About what?

WALTER: Look, I love the Beatles too, but . . . I mean, Phoebe just left you and all you can talk about is the Fab Four.

BEN: That's what the whole argument was about.

WALTER: No, the fight was about the fact that you're obsessed with a band that broke up in 1969.

BEN: 1970.

WALTER: My point exactly!

BEN: What are you saying?

WALTER: You need a little help from your friends.

BEN: *(Pause.)* Oh, that's not fair.

WALTER: No? then how 'bout "all you need is love"?

BEN: *(Pause.)* Right. Okay, yeah, you're right. Of course. Thank you.

WALTER: Any time. "I am you, as you are me, and we are all together."

BEN: No. It's "I am *he*, as you are me." Not "I am you." *(Slight pause.)* Get out of my house.

WALTER: Ben —

BEN: NO! You can call me crazy, you can take Phoebe's side, but when you twist the words of the Beatles to suit your own purposes, that's when I want you out.

WALTER: Okay, shut up and listen! *(Slight pause.)* You think marriage is tough? You think trying to live with another person — love their good points and accept their failings — is hard? Try divorce. *(Slight pause.)* I know what you're going through. You get married and things are great. You and Phoebe are happy. But then you start to disagree about money or when to have kids, and suddenly everything's a problem. Everyone says marriage isn't easy, but you didn't think it would be this hard, did you? *(Slight pause.)* Well, let me tell you . . . divorce . . . that's something that most mornings you can wake up and wonder if this'll be the day it all becomes too much, and you decide to step out that tenth floor window. *(Slight pause.)* So, you need to dig down in yourself and decide what it is you want in your life. And if Phoebe is something you want . . . then you're going to have to do some hard work. *(Pause.)* Do you know what you want?

BEN: *(Pause.)* You said Phoebe's at Elaine's?

WALTER: Yeah. *(Ben gets to his feet and quickly exits. Walter, worn out, sits. Blackout.)*

THE MYSTERY OF ATTRACTION
Marlane Meyer

Warren and Ray are brothers (twenties to thirties). Denise, Ray's wife, has just left, after busting Ray's hump. In walks Warren. This is the final scene in the play.

Warren comes in from the garden, stands looking at the front door.

WARREN: *(Beat.)* Wow. That was like watching a big boat sink. *(Warren makes drinks.)* You think maybe she has somebody . . . ? Just my observation with women is they walk out very easily when they've got somebody in their head, you know? Like when Sharky left so easily it was because I was in her head. You know? She had a sure thing, somebody she was sure of, so she was able to let you go, just like that . . .
(Ray groans loudly and comes at Warren in a rage, Warren ducks, eludes him. Ray is out of control, he screams incoherently.)

RAY: AHHHHHAHHAHHHHHHAHHAHAHHGHHGHHGHG-GHGHHGHAH . . .
(Warren catches him from behind and takes him down expertly, he holds him.)

WARREN: Breathe, breathe deeply and relax . . . relax! Come on! Give it up, big boy! Okay! Breathe, now! Come on!
(Warren is stronger and Ray relaxes and lies limply in his brother's arms.)

RAY: How do you fuck if you don't have a penis?

WARREN: I don't think you do.

RAY: I've heard of guys thinking they had their legs when their legs had been amputated, swearing they could feel their legs, but what about your dick, what happens?

WARREN: *(Thoughtfully.)* Well, it depends, I suppose on if they just take the dick.

RAY: Right. They could take the balls. I'd have no fluids . . . what do you think would happen . . . would my voice get higher . . . ?

WARREN: Stop it.

RAY: Seriously.

WARREN: It's not productive.

RAY: Will I be able to stop shaving?

WARREN: What are you doing?

RAY: Trying to look on the bright side.

WARREN: You know what you need? You need a job.

RAY: Maybe if they cut off my dick I could become a woman . . . get married. I wouldn't be able to have kids, the guy would have to love me for myself.

WARREN: Are you listening?

RAY: Did you ever see *Some Like It Hot?* Jack Lemmon dresses as a woman and by the end of the movie it looks like he's going to make a very good marriage to a millionaire played by Joe E. Brown.

WARREN: Look, all you need is one good case and you'd be clear of debt. What about this guy tonight . . . why don't you just take his case . . . this guy that was here with that . . .

RAY: Psychotic Gumdrop.

(Warren finds the check underneath some magazines on the table.)

WARREN: Look, here's this guy's check . . . for fifty thousand dollars.

(Warren keeps the check away.)

RAY: Gimme that . . . Warren?

WARREN: This is a large amount of money, it's more than you need.

RAY: Warren?!

WARREN: Rich people and their justice, Ray. It's all for sale. What's the case?

RAY: I'm not taking it.

WARREN: This girl killed somebody, right?

RAY: I don't remember.

WARREN: What have they got?

RAY: Plenty.

WARREN: Like what?

RAY: They have a signed confession, they have the knife.

WARREN: Okay, okay . . . well, you can get the confession bumped. *(Realizing.)* And I work in the evidence room.

RAY: Yeah, so?

WARREN: It doesn't take a genius to figure out why they chose you, Ray. This guy Larry knows about me, knows about you . . . why is that?

RAY: I don't know.

WARREN: It's a setup. Losing the knife. I can lose the knife.

RAY: No!

WARREN: Why not?

RAY: No, Warren! An act like this would change everything. It would change our lives in ways we can't even anticipate.

WARREN: Then what difference does it make? We're already off the train, we're already running in the dark . . .

RAY: You're talking about cooperating with human evil. That guy is evil, his daughter is damaged.

WARREN: Ray?

RAY: What?

WARREN: Who do we kill when we take a life?

RAY: Did you hear what I said?

WARREN: This is the argument you made against the death penalty and it worked, you got that guy life.

RAY: It doesn't apply here.

WARREN: Come on. Whose life do we take when we take a life?

RAY: *(Sigh.)* We take our own life.

WARREN: That's right. We take a piece of ourselves we've come to hate, we place it out there, on the face of an innocent person, and we murder that person, right? So, who dies?

RAY: Warren, I refuse to become involved in this.

WARREN: Ray, the girl was operating at her highest level of good, she was trying to the best of her ability to heal the war within herself by committing a murder, can't you understand that?

RAY: Yes, but it's still a murder, Warren.

WARREN: She's a young girl. She made a mistake.

RAY: This is not the first person she's killed? *(Beat.)*

WARREN: It's not?

RAY: No.

WARREN: Oh.

RAY: For God's sake, Warren, she needs to go away. I know you know this.

WARREN: No. I know.

RAY: I know the one thing we have in common is our love of justice.

WARREN: Okay, so there needs to be some kind of net in place is what you're saying.

RAY: Net?

WARREN: No, okay, I hear you. How about this? What if when she gets out, instead of just walking away she comes to us.

RAY: Us?

WARREN: Or me.

RAY: If she gets off, she'll be free. It's kind of not our problem at that point.

WARREN: But where is the justice in that?

RAY: That's what I'm saying . . . !

WARREN: But what if when she gets out, we keep her.

RAY: Keep her . . . ?

WARREN: I could keep her.

RAY: You mean, like kidnap her?

WARREN: Incarcerate.

RAY: That's insane.

WARREN: Every day people slip through the holes in the world because they have failed to learn the lessons of life. Failed to refine their sensibilities. Common courtesy is so uncommon as to be a joke. We are neck deep in human excrement wondering where to take our next crap. What is so insane about sequestering a rebellious and murdering girl?

RAY: Well, Warren, it's illegal for one thing.

WARREN: So is murder.

RAY: Warren, what is going on with you?

WARREN: I'll tell you, Ray. Sharky has driven me mad. She has tried to fix what is not broken in me and changed the way I look at myself and now I'm permanently screwed up. What's the little girl's name?

RAY: Vicky.

WARREN: I want to heal my relationship with women through my incarceration of Vicky.

RAY: How did we get here?

WARREN: It's become a twofold plan. I'll lock her up for murder but I'll rehabilitate her for me.

RAY: Will you take pictures of her?

WARREN: If I deem it part of the therapeutic process.

RAY: And for how long will you sequester this rebellious and murdering girl?

WARREN: Seven years, a cycle of time, but maybe, if she's amenable, forever.

RAY: Who's going to take care of her again?

WARREN: We will. Or I will. That will be my job. You will have to get some kind of a job and support us. Because I'll be fired, and I'll just stay home. Like a housewife taking care of the kids. She'll be like a daughter to us, you and me.

RAY: Yes, I'm married to my brother, we have one child.

WARREN: Think about it. Wouldn't it be great to have a kid?

RAY: I am thinking about it. Why am I thinking about this? It's crazy . . .

WARREN: Because crazier things happen all the time.

RAY: It's because I'm afraid.

WARREN: Sure. You're afraid of these evil men that have pulled you into a world of darkness . . .

RAY: Stop talking for minute, okay?

WARREN: I am trying to save your life.

RAY: Losing evidence can't be that easy. You will be found out, you will be punished. Right?

WARREN: Right . . . So, I have to have an excuse. For instance, you can be on drugs. Drugs are the obvious choice, especially with a cop like me who has a history of abuse. So, I'll get high and lose the knife.

RAY: And it's just a coincidence you lose the evidence on my case?

WARREN: You don't take the case.

RAY: I don't?

WARREN: Anybody could take the case.

RAY: But I keep the money . . . ?

WARREN: You fixed it.

RAY: And you'd do this for me?

WARREN: Yes.

RAY: Why? Why would you do such a thing for me? Give up a job you love, I mean, eventually you would get your old job back.

WARREN: I know that.

RAY: So why would you give that up?

WARREN: You're my brother.

RAY: No. Why really?

WARREN: That's it.

RAY: No, really.

WARREN: I want you to forgive me. For Sharky.

RAY: I have forgiven you, Warren, I couldn't do anything else but forgive
you . . . I love you.

WARREN: No, you don't understand.

RAY: Tell me.

WARREN: When Sharky came home and started to scream I struck her not
in anger so much as surprise. And she fell into the glass door and
thrashing to keep from falling ended up cutting herself even worse,
in fact, she punctured an artery.
(Ray sits down.)

RAY: Jesus.

WARREN: She was asking me to help but I couldn't . . . I saw what was
happening, but I couldn't seem to consider it an emergency. How
could I? It was a triumph. I was finally on level ground. She was so
weak and pathetic that all my hatred came out and I remained absolutely motionless and watched her dying. Her screaming turned
to begging and the begging finally turned to crying till finally . . .
and this is how I found out she still loved you . . . when she realized
she was going to die, she asked me to tell you that she had always
loved you, that there was never anyone else in her heart. And then,
she apologized to me, she did . . . *(Smiles.)* She apologized which I
must admit, felt good. That broke the spell, the apology. When she
did that I tried to help her, but by then it was too late. She was gone.
(Ray looks around, at loose ends.)
She told me she wasn't trying to fix me, she was trying to make me
more like you. Isn't that sweet?

RAY: Where is she?

WARREN: *(Moves to the garden.)* I put her out there. Out there under the
plumeria and the gardenia, where the jasmine is in bloom, where the
garden smells the sweetest. I put her out there for you. Deep in the
rich fragrant earth. She'll be mother to your garden, nurturing it for

years to come, if you leave her alone. Can you do that, Ray? Can you let her rest in peace?

RAY: *(Pause.)* Just like that? No funeral?

WARREN: We can have a funeral, we just can't invite anybody.

RAY: *(Beat.)* No.

WARREN: Think about it.

RAY: I thought of her every day. Warren, woke up thinking about her every day. Last thing on my mind at night. First thing in the morning. I still carry her picture in my wallet so when someone I don't know and never expect to see again asks to see a picture of my wife I show them Sharky and pretend we're still married, and that she's at home, waiting for me at home . . . the love of my life waiting for me to come home but I can never go home to her now, can I . . . ?

WARREN: Ray, you could have gone home to her anytime. You knew she was unhappy. Why didn't you call her up? One little phone call from you and I'll bet the drugs, the gambling, the human misery, all this, could have been avoided.

RAY: *(Beat.)* Are you . . . blaming me?

WARREN: In part.

RAY: *(Beat.)* Right. Okay. I can see your point. I do see it. *(Beat.)* But I'm still calling the police on you . . . you amoral shithead.
(Ray goes toward the phone, Warren gets there first, takes the phone and moves away.)

WARREN: Can I say one more thing?

RAY: Give me the phone.

WARREN: If you leave her there in the garden, she'll always be there to come home to.

RAY: Warren?
(Warren hands him the phone.)

WARREN: I know, it's not the happiest ending . . . but at least we're to-gether, Ray. It's a way of looking at it, I don't know if you can ap-preciate the symmetry, but it's there. You have what many people long for with their ex's. Closure.

RAY: How can you ask me to do this?

WARREN: Because we're lost men, Ray. And all we have is each other.
(The two men watch each other for a long beat. Blackout.)

SCENE AT MOUNT RUSHMORE
Quincy Long

Bobby and Did are two brothers. They are visiting Mt. Rushmore. Both
are in their twenties.

Bobby and his brother Did gaze upwards.

BOBBY: That sure looks like her, don't it, Did?

DID: Looks like who, Bobby?

BOBBY: Like Momma.

DID: What?

BOBBY: Second from the left there. Looks like Momma with her hair down.

DID: Them is men, Bobby.

Boddy: Who?

DID: All of them up there. They's presidents. And presidents is men. So
far anyways.

BOBBY: Sure look like Momma to me.

DID: I ain't paying you no attention, Bobby. I am here to see my presidents in stone; to contemplate my country how it used to be.

BOBBY: Maybe Momma was a man.

DID: I'm a pop you one you keep this up.

BOBBY: Oh, hey now.

DID: You ain't changed a bit, Bobby. Always making fun. Woman dead
and in the ground and here you are making fun.

BOBBY: I ain't making fun, Did. I see her up there. I see her everywhere
I look. Only reason you don't, you didn't grieve her when she died,
which is why you can't see it.

DID: I grieved our momma.

BOBBY: Nah you didn't. You got up and read out of the Book. And you
read good, real good. I'd be a liar I didn't own I was jealous the way
you stuck out. But you did not grieve our momma, and I think you

should, Did, because, my humble opinion, that's the trouble with Janney.

DID: Oh, now it's my wife now.

BOBBY: No, I admire your wife, Did. She's a good woman. A handsome woman. And a cook in the kitchen too. But how she come to get so fat? You ever ask yourself?

DID: That ain't fat, that's wholesome looking.

BOBBY: When the floor groans underneath of your weight, Did, that is fat. And Janney is fat because of she eats too much. I seen it. And she eats too much because of how you run her down. I hear it. And you run her down because you ain't grieved your momma. I know it.

DID: Oh boy oh boy oh boy. You is and always was the pure momma's boy wasn't you?

BOBBY: You can't hurt me with that.

DID: Always the little helper at the grocery. Picking up the basket. Toting it to the house. Wiping down the milk. Momma's regular little chore girl.

BOBBY: Can't nobody hurt me no more with that old slam. I come to peace with who I am. I traced it and faced it, brother.

DID: Well, goody for you.

BOBBY: Remember the time you and Daddy was back of the barn with that axle to lift, and I come to help you, and you shooed me out of there?

DID: Hell, I don't know.

BOBBY: Groaning and sweating in your undershirts. I remember it like tomorrow.

DID: Yesterday, Bobby.

BOBBY: What?

DID: You remember it like it was yesterday.

BOBBY: Yes I do. Did. The mortification of it. The shame. That I was not allowed, not invited to participate with the work of the farm. That I was not fit somehow to be a part of it.

DID: You wasn't but a little kid back then.

BOBBY: I was old enough, Did. But I come to terms with all that. Since I left the farm I come to realize that lifting axles up off the ground is not in my line. I been called to another portion. My talents is more toward lifting the heavy load of sorrow from off the shoulders of my fellow man, up to and including my brother Diddie if it needs be.

DID: Well, I'm glad to see you found yourself, Bobby. And I appreciate the concern. And maybe I am just a disappointed sinner with a fat wife. But how that comes of not grieving a woman I never did love, that I cannot understand.

BOBBY: Oh, Did.

DID: No. No. You think because she took me to a bathing beach once I should grieve her? You think because she made me Pork Chop Sizzle for my birthday once I should grieve her? You think because I come out between of her particular legs instead of a million billion other women in the world I should grieve her? Well I don't. I reject that as the philosophy of an emotional person.

BOBBY: She was your one and only momma, Did.

DID: But I didn't know her, Bobby. You grieve the ones you know, and the woman was nothing but a mystery to me.

BOBBY: She was a mystery to herself what I come to understand.

DID: Well, I'm sorry for that. And I'm sorry she died before her time. And I'm sorry I didn't love her like I should of, but dang it all Bobby —

BOBBY: Did you know she died with your name in her mouth?

DID: What?

BOBBY: Died calling for Did. For her first born, yeah.

DID: Who told you that?

BOBBY: Daddy.

DID: No.

BOBBY: He called me drunk one night.

DID: Well, he's liable to say anything drunk.

BOBBY: No, he told me things. Other things. How she'd never wanted children. The farm. The dirt. The work. The worry. None of it.

DID: Oh, and that's what I'm supposed to grieve, huh? Some stoney woman never wanted me? Never calls me 'til she's dead? That's what I'm a supposed to cry big crockababy tears about?

BOBBY: That's it, Did. That's the job.

DID: Well I ain't up to it.

BOBBY: Yeah you are. Sure you are. Look at them presidents all carved out of rock. You think whoever done that woke up every morning happy

to climb a mountain? But he done it. And died doing it. And his
son carried it on. That's what we do here. We got no choice in it.

DID: Ain't I glad I invited you along on my once-a-year vacation.

BOBBY: I was touched you asked me, Did.

DID: Well I may never again, but I grant you one thing, Bobby Lee.

BOBBY: What's that?

DID: Goddamn if that don't begin to look a bit like Momma now the
light has shifted.

BOBBY: That's funny, brother.

DID: What?

BOBBY: Because I don't see it no more.

OTHER PEOPLE
Christopher Shinn

Stephen and Mark are both in their twenties. Stephen has invited Mark, his ex-boyfriend, to visit for Christmas. Mark has recently completed an indie film. He is also fresh out of rehab.

Lights rise on Stephen on his loft bed, Mark on the couch on the phone.

MARK: — Well yeah. I can come in, well. Um. You should. *(Petra exits the apartment. Stephen looks up from his bed.)* Well like I said I'll have to. Oh? Well I suppose this is all. Great, especially for. Well I can come in I can. Anytime. Okay. That's fine. But like I said. 'Til I see it. Okay. Yeah. 'Til I. Well that's great that people are. But like I said. Okay. Okay that's fine. Okay. Bye.
(He hangs up the phone. He opens up a book. Stephen climbs off his loft bed, grabs his coat from the closet, enters the living room.)

STEPHEN: Hey.

MARK: Oh. Hi.

STEPHEN: Hey thanks again for dinner.

MARK: Oh. You're welcome but, I have all this money.

STEPHEN: Yeah. I was gonna — oh, whatcha reading?

MARK: The Bible.

STEPHEN: *(Laughs.)* Ha. *(Stops.)* Oh — the Bible, really?

MARK: The Good Book.

STEPHEN: The Good News Bible.

MARK: The King James version.

STEPHEN: Right. Right. Um. Well I was going to go down to the deli and get my self a Snapple or — how are you feeling, you want anything?

MARK: I'm fine.

STEPHEN: Snapple has this new peach juice which is — anyway, I'm just, I'm just going to *say* this however foreign to my nature it is to speak *directly, honestly,* you know, but, that's one of the things I've been working on, so. So, I just: I want to know you're okay. I guess. You've been really quiet, and . . .

MARK: I'm fine. Really. I know I'm. I know this is. Different. Unlikely even.

STEPHEN: Well yeah! Very — it's definitely a — *new you* here, ha.

MARK: With the help of the Lord, yes. A new. Me. *(Pause.)*

STEPHEN: I'm just, I'm a little uneasy, it's been so long you know and I feel a little — *lost* with you — and of course, our history, you know, and — your coming back here without our discussing — what's really *happened* in the — in the time you've been — gone — *you* — you not being something we've discussed and why — when you could stay anywhere why — I mean I knew it was a rough time so I didn't want to push but — now — just to know — what's going through your head.

MARK: Right. Well. I think you'll find I tend to be more — silent and not. Interested. In the past. Because. It causes me pain to think about it. My life is about. The new me. In so many ways. In this way *(Holds up the Bible.)* especially.

STEPHEN: Right. Right, well. And that's great, that's what you needed to — recover. And I understand, I guess I'm just being selfish, you know Petra's the same way. She was in Japan for over half a year, you know, stripping, and she's finally given it up, you know, she saved a lot of money and she's come back so now she has money to write and to — do what she wants without having to — you know, and which is *great* — and she's the same, not wanting to — *talk,* to *define* herself based on — so. So. It's hard for *me* but I understand.

MARK: The past is — bad news. It's only good news now. For me. And thank God. Thank God.

STEPHEN: Right, sure. It's just so — different. But — well — hell you know — maybe we're all — getting it together, which is great. Like our apartment is about *health* you know, *healthy* living —we're all — being *proactive* — not to sound not to sound New Agey but . . .

MARK: You don't sound New Agey.

STEPHEN: Right, well, we're making *improvements.*

MARK: Absolutely. God bless us. It's not easy. This world.

STEPHEN: Yeah! Yeah, and I guess, and it doesn't have to be now, I guess though I just hope we will you know eventually have a chance to *talk,* really *talk*, about the past year and — you know? just to — and — well maybe I thought — I'd feel better if I — if we — hugged, I mean we haven't because — I do love you, not, not in the past way but in this new way, you know?

MARK: Change is traumatic. It will take getting used to. The past me, Stephen. That's someone else. Have faith in. This me. Have faith in me now and know all will. Will be all right.

STEPHEN: Right.

MARK: I'll give you a hug.

STEPHEN: Good. *(Mark stands, hugs Stephen briefly, breaks the hug.)*

MARK: You're my only friend. Only true, real friend in this world. I was too terrified to go at it alone, to jump back into the. Real world. Without you. God bless you. I say prayers of thanks that I am here with you.

STEPHEN: Right, right, well great. *(The phone rings.)*

MARK: Oh, give me some peace! Let the voice mail get it.

STEPHEN: Who are these, are these the movie people?

MARK: Yes. Oh, Stephen. I have the option — because most of what was used ended up being mine — of putting my name on the film. Which I haven't — seen. This is. A dilemma.

STEPHEN: Oh.

MARK: They're sending me the cut. It doesn't really matter. The Lord will guide me.

STEPHEN: Right. Um — well I have to get going on these *blurbs* I — I hope I didn't — upset you or — I just get neurotic, still, I hate it.

MARK: Then give it up. Release yourself to the Holy Spirit. What's "neurotic"? What is that? Hand it to God, he'll know what to do with it. It won't be easy. But you can do it.

STEPHEN: Yeah. Yeah. God, it's a Marianne Williamson moment! Right — well — you're probably right. I'm just — so proud of you. And Petra. And glad you'll be getting to know each other, I always kept you two apart, I kept my life so compartmentalized before, you know. Well I'll let you back to your reading. God, when I was a kid, I was into this totally weird Wiccan stuff. — Anyway. You want anything from the deli?

MARK: I don't need anything.

STEPHEN: Okay. *(Stephen goes to the door.)* Um. And just anytime you need anything. *Anything.* I am here for you.

MARK: Thank you.

STEPHEN: Anything at all. Just knock on my door. Anytime no matter what. I want you to be well.

MARK: I will be. And God bless you.

STEPHEN: Right. Okay. Just — wanted to say that. So. Off to get my Snapple!

(Stephen goes. Mark opens the Bible.)

TAPE
Stephen Belber

Jon and Vincent are both in their thirties, high school buddies who haven't seen each other in years. Jon is an aspiring filmmaker. Vince is a small time drug dealer and volunteer fireman who is obsessed with the memory of a girl Jon "stole" from him in high school. Vince believes that Jon raped this girl and is trying to get him to admit it.

JON: *(Beat.)* Funny how you get this way every time we talk about Amy Randall.

VINCENT: No I don't.

JON: I don't even think you realize it, Vince.

VINCENT: Fuck off.

JON: OK, you know what? — I'm outta here —

VINCENT: Fuck off.

JON: Thanks for coming —

VINCENT: Fuck off —

JON: Vincent.

VINCENT: Fuck *you,* Jon! —

JON: Look — I'm sorry you still feel bad about Amy Randall, and that every time you get stoned and drunk around me this comes up. But it was ten years ago; I've explained to you a million times that I felt that it was OK for me to be with her because you guys had broken up, and that I now have a better understanding as to the *fragility* of human emotions — especially those belonging to swarthy Italian-Americans like yourself — and thus if the situation arose again today, I wouldn't let what happened happen. But these things *do* happen, especially in high school, and I'm sorry I hurt your feelings.

VINCENT: *(Pause.)* That's not what I'm talking about.

JON: What're you talking about?

VINCENT: I'm talking about what happened.

JON: So am I.

VINCENT: So what happened?

JON: We slept together.

VINCENT: How?

JON: What do you mean?

VINCENT: How did you sleep together?

JON: OK — so now this is about that?

VINCENT: Isn't it?

JON: Is it?

VINCENT: *You* tell *me.*

JON: We slept together.

VINCENT: How?

JON: You *know* how.

VINCENT: No, actually, I don't. I have an idea, but I don't *know* because we've never actually *talked* about it. We've *laughed* about it; we thought it was kinda *funny,* but you've never exactly *told* me what happened.

JON: So what do you wanna know?

VINCENT: I wanna know what happened.

JON: We slept together.

VINCENT: How?

JON: What do you mean "how"?

VINCENT: *How!*

JON: You have to be more specific, Vince.

VINCENT: In what fashion did you sleep with her?

JON: We had sex.

VINCENT: And — ?

JON: And that was it.

VINCENT: Was it good sex?

JON: I've had better since.

VINCENT: Was it on the rough side?

JON: Hard to say. We were both drunk.

VINCENT: Did you rape her?

JON: *(Beat . . . Thinks he's joking.)* No.

VINCENT: Kind of?

JON: No!

VINCENT: Was it like date rape?

JON: "*Like* date rape"?

VINCENT: Did you "kind of" force her to have sex with you?

JON: No!!

(Silence.)

VINCENT: Jon?

JON: I'm not sure what you want me to say, Vince.

VINCENT: I want you to tell me what happened. *You're* a filmmaker —
lay out the scene for me — show me the dailies.

JON: Can we talk about this sometime when you're not high?

VINCENT: Maybe the only reason I'm high is so that *you* get high so that
for once you can tell me the truth instead of changing the subject.

JON: *(Beat.)* Yes, it was a little rough. Which is obviously something that
doesn't make me proud.

VINCENT: *(Beat.)* Did you ever talk to her after that?

JON: No.

VINCENT: Why not?

JON: Because I wouldn't know what to say to her. I'm a completely different person than I was then.

VINCENT: Maybe she is too.

JON: May-be.

VINCENT: Maybe she's fat.

JON: That's really not funny.

VINCENT: I didn't say it was. *(Beat.)* Does anyone else know what happened?

JON: *I* didn't tell anyone.

VINCENT: Maybe you should.

JON: I don't actually consider it a crime, Vince. It was not a good thing,
it was morally somewhat questionable and I wish it hadn't happened,
but I don't think it's the type of thing where I need to turn myself
into the police ten years later.

VINCENT: I'm not talking about the police.

JON: So what're you talking about?

VINCENT: I dunno. Her.

JON: I think she already knows.

VINCENT: Maybe you should apologize.

JON: Oh Jesus —

VINCENT: What?

JON: You want me to *apologize* to her?

VINCENT: Why not?

JON: It wasn't even date rape, Vince! — It was just something that got a little out of hand —

VINCENT: I thought you weren't sure what date rape was.

JON: Look — I'm sorry.

VINCENT: Don't apologize to me.

JON: *(Recomposing.)* I'm not. What I'm trying to say is that ten years ago I did something wrong, and when I think about it now, it seems like the person who did that is a complete stranger to me. A dumb, drunk, high-school senior who thought she was just being a little prudish and needed some coercion. It was bad and I regret it but it was a far cry from rape. And I don't think *she* would look back on it and call it that either.

VINCENT: What *would* she call it —

JON: I don't know what she'd call it? —

VINCENT: What if she called it rape? —

JON: Listen to me, I highly, highly doubt that she even remembers it —

VINCENT: *You* remember it —

JON: I remember it because it was a pivotal thing for me —

VINCENT: Your *first* rape?

JON: Stop being an asshole —

VINCENT: Tell me why it was pivotal.

JON: Because it was one of the first times I looked at myself objectively and decided that I would try to avoid becoming a certain type of person. OK? For her it might have been nothing particularly important one way or another; for me, it constituted something more significant.

VINCENT: So you'd like to think.

JON: Why are you suddenly high and mighty? —

VINCENT: I'm not high and mighty — I'm too *high* to be high and mighty! I'm just a lowly, drug-dealing, boxer-wearing scum of the earth.

JON: You said it —

VINCENT: No, actually, *you* did —

JON: I didn't mean it like that —

VINCENT: How'd you mean it? —

JON: That you should change your life a bit —

VINCENT: This coming from a rapist —

JON: You're an idiot —

VINCENT: Sorry — this coming from a big low-budget moviemaker who makes movies about "where society is possibly headed if we can just manage to forget about that date rape we didn't *kind of* really commit in high school."

JON: You're seriously disturbed.

VINCENT: No, actually, I *am* high and mighty. I was wrong before.

JON: What do you want me to say, Vince? — I'm sorry.

VINCENT: Stop apologizing to *me,* Jon —

JON: I'm not! I'm apologizing in general. I wish it had never happened. I don't think I'm an evil person.

VINCENT: No one's saying you're evil —

JON: It sure as hell feels like it —

VINCENT: Do *you* think you're evil?

JON: No —

VINCENT: So then you're not evil. *I'm* the evil one here. You're the morally conscious moviemaker.

JON: Whatever —

VINCENT: Whatever —

JON: Can we stop now? —

VINCENT: Totally —

JON: Thank you —

VINCENT: *(Beats . . .)* I just think you should call her.

JON: I'm not gonna call her.

VINCENT: I think you should —

JON: Stop! OK? To call her would be to trivialize the entire matter. It would be like saying, "How's life — oh by the way, sorry I date-raped you ten years ago."

VINCENT: So you *did* date-rape her?

JON: No, I didn't —

VINCENT: What *did* you do?

JON: I coerced her to have sex with me.

VINCENT: How?

JON: Verbally.

VINCENT: You verbally coerced her?

JON: Yes. *(Pause.)* By applying excessive linguistic pressure, I persuaded her to have sex with me.

VINCENT: And *then* things got rough?

JON: Things got rough in that after awhile they become aggressively playful.

VINCENT: *They* did?

JON: We did.

VINCENT: Meaning what?

JON: Meaning I probably still thought I was being playful but others might interpret my actions as being rough.

VINCENT: — i.e., rape.

JON: No — rough.

VINCENT: Look — Jon, only you two know what happened, so only you two can "interpret" your actions. So why don't you just tell me the facts and interpret them later.

JON: I'm telling you — I argued her into it —

VINCENT: You're fucking, *lying,* Jon! *(Silence.)*

JON: What is your problem?

VINCENT: How can you sit here with your oldest friend in the world and continuously tell lies?

JON: What makes you think I'm lying?

VINCENT: Because only *you* would come up with the term, "excessive linguistic pressure." That's not a normal expression, Jon, it's a clear sign of excessive bullshit. If you had really done only that, you'd be more specific. You'd say that you told her that if she didn't put out you'd start telling people she had V.D. or smelled bad, or had a penis, or any of the *normal* things that guys say. But *you* come up with your typical crap, which *sounds* mature but contains *nothing!* But it's bullshit, because the reason you are where you are today is because you always insist on getting things your way. It's what you're good at, Jon, so why don't you just own up and admit what you did?!

JON: *(Beat.)* Fuck off, Vince. *(Jon heads for the door.)*

VINCENT: Fine. *I'll* call her. *(Vince reaches for the phone.)*

JON: Don't do that.

VINCENT: Why not? —

JON: Because I would like you not to —

VINCENT: Why not? —

JON: Because you're already made your point —

VINCENT: What's my point? —

JON: Your point is that nobody's perfect, including me, so it offends you when I tell you how I think you should live your life.

VINCENT: That's not my point —

JON: It should be —

VINCENT: It's not —

JON: Why? —

VINCENT: Because I haven't gotten to my point yet —

JON: So then get to it —

VINCENT: Maybe I don't have one —

JON: Then I'm gonna go —

VINCENT: Wrong —

JON: No — right.

(Jon starts for the door but Vince beats him to it. Vince locks the door and stands firmly in front of it.)

VINCENT: Admit it.

JON: Admit what?

VINCENT: What you did to Amy.

JON: What even makes you think I did something?

VINCENT: Because I know —

JON: How? —

VINCENT: Because she told me —

JON: Told you what? —

VINCENT: What you did —

JON: What did she say?

VINCENT: . . . Nothing.

JON: Get outta my way, Vincent.

VINCENT: It was obvious —

(Jon reaches for the door handle only to have Vince shove him forcefully in the chest. The confrontation has reached a whole new level.)

VINCENT: Tell me what you did and I'll let you go.

JON: Stop being a dick —

VINCENT: Tell me what you did —

JON: Why do you care?

VINCENT: 'Cause I wanna hear it —

JON: What would that change?

VINCENT: I don't know! —

JON: So then what does it matter? — we both know I did something wrong! —

VINCENT: So then tell me! —

JON: I pinned her arms back and stuck my dick in! OK?! For Christ fucking sakes! Shit happens! I already said I'm sorry! *(Silence . . .)*

VINCENT: Thank you. *(Vince steps away from Jon, goes to his duffel bag, reaches inside and carefully rummages around for a second. Jon looks on with exhaustion and curiosity. After a moment, Vince takes out a small tape recorder from the bag. He looks at it briefly to make sure it is still running, then presses the "stop" button. He then places the tape recorder on the floor in front of him. Beat. Jon, having registered the import of this, stares at the recorder, and then at Vince. More silence.)*

JON: What the hell did you just do?

VINCENT: Taped our conversation.

JON: *(Pause.)* Why?

VINCENT: I wanted to make sure I heard you right. *(Beat; Vince picks up the recorder, presses "rewind" briefly, then presses "play." Tape: "I pinned her arms back and stuck my dick in! OK?! For Christ fucking sakes! Shit happens!" Vince presses "stop." Beat.)* I guess you're right — you *are* a completely different person.

JON: *(Hollow shock.)* I can't believe you just did that.

(Vince now takes a sticker label for the tape and writes on it, then methodically places the label onto the tape. He then puts the tape in the pocket of his pants, which lay strewn on the bed. He puts his pants on. He then goes to his bag once more and takes out two beers.)

VINCENT: Beer?

THE TEST
Paula J. Caplan

Cleveland and Bradley are both black men in their twenties. *The Test* takes place in a prison, on death row. Cleveland is trying to teach Bradley to read.

> *Cleveland and Bradley are onstage, seated. Bradley holds a Bible and is reading from it. When reading, Bradley is slow and takes frequent pauses to work it out.*

BRADLEY: Yuh . . . eeee. *(Beat.)* Yuh-ee, yee!

CLEVELAND: Close.

BRADLEY: Not yee?

CLEVELAND: Why do you say it's yee?

BRADLEY: It starts with "y," and then there's "e" "a," and you said "e" "a" sounds like "ee" like in "eat."

CLEVELAND: You know, you're right. That's good. But sometimes "e" "a" sounds like "say."

BRADLEY: Not another one. Why can't a rule ever be a rule? Why is there always "but sometimes the rule's no good"?

CLEVELAND: That's just how it is. I know it's hard.

BRADLEY: So this is . . .

CLEVELAND: It's "yay." Go on.

BRADLEY: *(Reading, pronouncing "Yea" correctly.)* "Yea . . . thog. Yea, thog . . ."

CLEVELAND: This "g" is silent, and so is the "h."

BRADLEY: "Yea, thou"?

CLEVELAND: Well, that's a good Bible word, but this one is "though. Yea though." Go on.

BRADLEY: "Yea, though I walk" — it's walk, isn't it? *(Beat.)* "throw . . ."

CLEVELAND: "through. I walk through . . ."

BRADLEY: "through the . . . val-ley of the sha . . . um . . . sha-dow, shadow! . . . of . . .um, daith"? It's "e" then "a" like "yea," so daith?

CLEVELAND: It's "death." You sure chose a hard psalm.

BRADLEY: Yes, but . . .

CLEVELAND: I know. I know. *(Beat.)* Hey, don't feel bad, man. I can't believe how far you've come. Words like "Adam" and "Eve" and "Eden" and even "snake" are lots easier than these. Six months ago you couldn't do those, and now you breeze right through them. This stuff today is really, really difficult. Want to take a short break?

BRADLEY: OK. *(Beat.)* I don't know why you help me so much.

CLEVELAND: I'll help anyone who wants that much to learn. 'Specially this book. That's my thing in here, Bradley. My whole purpose is to help guys who want to read better. And read this better.

BRADLEY: It's not stupid to try to learn now?

CLEVELAND: Any more than me trying to teach now?

BRADLEY: You got me there. We'll both be dead before Easter.

CLEVELAND: You might not. Not with your new one.

BRADLEY: Man, she's a fighter, ain't she? She was here this morning.

CLEVELAND: Any news?

BRADLEY: Um, yeah, I forgot to tell you. The judge says I've got to get the test.

CLEVELAND: *The* test? No joke?

BRADLEY: Right. A psy-chiatrist is coming tomorrow to give it to me.

CLEVELAND: I think it's a psychologist who gives that kind of test.

BRADLEY: What's the difference?

CLEVELAND: *(Answering the question but actually focusing on the news.)* Psychiatrists are shrink doctors. Psychologists are called "Dr. Something" but they're not doctor-doctors. They do the tests to see how smart you are.

BRADLEY: They want to see if I'm dumb enough they should fry me?

CLEVELAND: No, Bradley. They didn't tell you?

BRADLEY: Tell me what?

CLEVELAND: The test is because if you're *not* smart they *can't* electrocute you.

BRADLEY: Why not? I killed the guy.

CLEVELAND: Yes, but you thought he was hurting your mother.

BRADLEY: Yes, I did. And I thought she was yelling because she wanted him to stop. And everybody said I was a dumb-ass 'cause I didn't know.

CLEVELAND: I know. So now you've finally got a lawyer who really listened. And she believes you. See, Bradley, lots of guys woulda know that wasn't why your ma was yelling. And Ms. Jules told the judge she can prove you didn't understand. You really thought you were helping your mother. The test will show that you didn't hurt him for a *mean* reason. And then the law says they can't kill you.

BRADLEY: She said something about they can't, but she's so nice I just thought she didn't want me to feel sad.

CLEVELAND: No, she was telling the truth. Bradley, this is wonderful!

BRADLEY: So the test is they'll ask why I killed that guy? I'll get to say I didn't mean to be mean?

CLEVELAND: No. The test is to find out how smart you are.

BRADLEY: *(Sad.)* Aw, no! No way I can pass that test.

CLEVELAND: *(Not noticing Bradley is sad.)* Whoa, there *is* a God! And he is good!

BRADLEY: They always put me in the dumbest group. In fifth grade I was the only one in "Spiders" group for reading. No way I can pass.

CLEVELAND: *(Realizing Bradley doesn't get it.)* Bradley, listen to me. You don't *want* to pass this test. This is the one time it's *good* to flunk a test. Good? Hey, it's great!

BRADLEY: It's *good* to flunk?

CLEVELAND: Listen to me, Bradley. Your reading has gotten so much better.

BRADLEY: Thanks to you, my man!

CLEVELAND: But listen. That means it will be easier for you to read the questions on the test and know some right answers.

BRADLEY: Yeah!

CLEVELAND: So you can be sure to give *wrong* answers.

BRADLEY: Give wrong answers?

CLEVELAND: Yes, Bradley. You *need* to flunk.

BRADLEY: I *need* to flunk?

CLEVELAND: Yes. For this test, it is good to flunk.

BRADLEY: Good to flunk??! Hallelujah!

CLEVELAND: Hallelujah, baby!

(They dance gloriously.)

CLEVELAND: Man, if they tested you for dancing, you'd be at the top of the class!

BRADLEY: Yeah, music was the good part of school. *(Rapping and dancing, first makes rap rhythm sounds with no words, then begins with the words.)* Yo, bro', didja hear, didja hear about the test?

CLEVELAND: *(Joining the dancing and rapping.)* No, man, I never heard, never heard about the test.

BRADLEY: It's the test, it's the test where the worst is the best!

CLEVELAND: It's the test, it's the test where the worst is the best!

(They make more rap rhythm sounds with no words, then resume the words.)

BRADLEY: I'd never thunk that it's *good* to flunk!

CLEVELAND: You'd never thunk that it's good to flunk?

BRADLEY: And if I fail,

CLEVELAND: And if you fail . . .

BRADLEY: I'll get *out* of jail! I'll get *out* of jail!

(Bradley goes on alone with rap rhythm sounds and goes on dancing alone, but Cleveland stops.)

CLEVELAND: Brad, my man, wait. You gotta know this. If you fail the test, you won't die in the chair, but they might not let you out. It just depends.

BRADLEY: Oh. Yeah. Depends on the judge?

CLEVELAND: I don't know for sure. Maybe a judge. Maybe another jury trial. Ask Ms. Jules.

(Silence.)

BRADLEY: But wait! Hey, that's OK! Just me not dyin' would mean so much to Ma. *(Beat.)* And, then, if I know I'm gonna live, I can do a lot of stuff in *here*. *(Beat.)* I'll get me a band together!

CLEVELAND: That'd be great. Bradley, it's gonna happen. I know it. It's gonna happen.

(A celebratory hand clasp between them.)

BRADLEY: But. Aw, no. But you . . . I mean . . . even if I get off, there ain't gonna be a test for you, right? Cause they know you'd never flunk.

CLEVELAND: Right. But this minute, Bradley, I'm so happy for you I don't care about me. I've known for a long time there was no way out for me.

BRADLEY: Hold on! That's what I thought about me. But look now! I know, I'll talk to Ms. Jules about you. She's so damn smart I know she can think of something.

CLEVELAND: You're a good man, Bradley. Thank you. But it doesn't really matter. See, the guy I killed, it wasn't like with your Ma. I killed him because I thought no one was home when I went to rob his house, and suddenly he was there with a gun. And, well, I had a gun because . . . I always had one. And I've always been hotheaded.

BRADLEY: Your head is hot?

CLEVELAND: Huh? Oh, not really hot. It means it's real easy to get me mad. Bradley, when I killed that guy, I wasn't trying to help anyone. I knew *exactly* what I was doing. It's taken me fifteen years, but I've found the Lord, and I'm ready to go. I've made my peace with God. All I want is to know you're going to live. No foolin'. Because you weren't out for yourself. You never meant to hurt anybody.

BRADLEY: But Cleve, I shoulda known. I should known. If I hadn't been so stupid I would've. It ain't like I didn't know about . . . I mean, *I'd* even . . . it's just, I'd never seen Ma like that. And she'd always helped me, told me I didn't need to be smart, just try my best.

CLEVELAND: It's good that she did that, Bradley.

BRADLEY: Yeah, she said as long as I tried hard, I shouldn't worry about smart or dumb. That made me feel better. And I never got to do nothin' to help her. So when I saw . . . I didn't get into my dumb head what it was. Stupid. My whole damn life. Stupid.

CLEVELAND: Bradley, the guard's coming. Give 'em hell tomorrow. Hey, maybe this is the one test you can enjoy! Huh?
(They slap hands.)

PERMISSION ACKNOWLEDGMENTS

A.M. SUNDAY by Jerome Hairston. Copyright 2002 by Jerome Hairston. Reprinted by permission of Rosenstone/Wender, 38 E. 29th St., New York, NY 10016. All rights reserved. The entire text of *A.M. Sunday* has been published by Smith and Kraus in *Humana Festival 2002: The Complete Plays.*

ARMITAGE by Don Nigro. Copyright 2002 by Don Nigro. Reprinted by permission of the author Samuel French, Inc., 45 W. 25th St., New York, NY 10010. All rights reserved. The entire text of *Armitage* has been published in an acting edition by Samuel French, Inc.

AS IT IS IN HEAVEN by Arlene Hutton. Copyright 2003 by Arlene Hutton. Reprinted by permission of Beacon Artists Agency, 630 9th Ave., #215, New York, NY 10036 (Attn: Pat McLaughlin). All rights reserved. The entire text of *As It Is In Heaven* has been published by Smith and Kraus in *Women Playwrights: The Best Plays of 2002* and in an acting edition by Dramatists Play Service.

BANG by Laura Shaine Cunningham. Copyright 2002 by Laura Shaine Cunningham. Reprinted by permission of Bret Adams Ltd., 448 W. 44th St., New York, NY 10036 (Attn: Bruce Ostler). All rights reserved. The entire texts of *Bang* and *Beautiful Bodies* are contained in *Plays by Laura Shaine Cunningham,* published by Broadway Play Publishing.

BEAST WITH TWO BACKS by Don Nigro. Copyright 1975, 1981, 2002 by Don Nigro. Reprinted by permission of the author and Samuel French, Inc., 45 W. 25th St., New York, NY 10010. All rights reserved. The entire text of *Beast With Two Backs* has been published in an acting edition of Samuel French, Inc.

BEAUTIFUL BODIES by Laura Shaine Cunningham. Copyright 2002 by Laura Shaine Cunningham. Reprinted by permission of Bret Adams Ltd., 448 W. 44th St., New York, NY 10036 (Attn: Bruce Ostler). All rights reserved. The entire texts of *Bang* and *Beautiful Bodies* are contained in *Plays by Laura Shaine Cunningham,* published by Broadway Play Publishing.

BINGO BABES by Isabel Duarte. Copyright 2000, 2002 by Isabel Duarte. Reprinted by permission of Samuel French, Inc. All rights reserved. The entire text of *Bingo Babes* has been published in an acting edition by Samuel French, Inc.

GOLDEN LADDER by Donna Spector. Copyright 2002 by Arlene Hutton. Reprinted by permission of Carolyn French, Fifi Oscard Assoc., 24 W. 40th St., 10th Fl., New York, NY 10018. All rights reserved. The entire text of *Golden Ladder* has been published by Smith and Kraus in *Women Playwrights: The Best Plays of 2002.*

GOOD THING by Jessica Goldberg. Copyright 2002 by Jessica Goldberg. Reprinted by permission of William Morris Agency, Inc., 1325 Ave. of the Americas, New York, NY 10019. All rights reserved. The entire text of *Good Thing* has been published in an acting edition by Dramatists Play Service.

THE GRADUATE by Terry Johnson. Copyright 2002 by Morgan Street Limited. Reprinted by permission of Sacha Brooks, Morgan Street Ltd., 55 Greek St., London W1D 3DT, Great Britain. All rights reserved. The entire text of *The Graduate* has been published in a trade edition by Methuen Publishing Ltd., and will be published in an acting edition at some unspecified future date by Samuel French, Inc.

LAST CALL by Kelly McAllister. Copyright 2002 by Kelly McAllister. Reprinted by permission of the author. All rights reserved. The entire text of *Last Call* has been published by NY Theatre Experience in *Plays and Playwrights 2003.*

LIMONADE TOUS LES JOURS by Charles L. Mee. Copyright 2001 by Charles L. Mee. Reprinted by permission of International Creative Management, 40 W. 57th St., New York, NY 10019 (Attn: Libby Edwards, assistant to Martin Kooij). All rights reserved. The entire text of *Limonade Tous Les Jours* has been published by Smith and Kraus in *Humana Festival 2002: The Complete Plays.*

MONTHS ON END by Craig Allan Pospisil. Copyright 2003 by Craig Pospisil. Reprinted by permission of Beacon Artists Agency, 630 9th Ave., New York, NY 10036. Attn: Pat McLaughlin. All rights reserved. The entire text of *Months on End* has been published in an acting edition by Dramatists Play Service.

THE MYSTERY OF ATTRACTION by Marlane Meyer. Copyright 2001 by Marlane Meyer. Reprinted by permission of John Buzzetti, The Gersh Agency, 41 Madison Ave., New York, NY 10010. All rights reserved. The entire text of *The Mystery of Attraction* has been published by Smith and Kraus in *Humana Festival 2002: The Complete Plays.* An acting edition of the play is to be published at some unspecified future date by Dramatists Play Service, 440 Park Ave. South,

New York, NY 10016, to whom all inquiries pertaining to stage production may be addressed. CAUTION: Professionals and amateurs are hereby warned that *The Mystery of Attraction* is subject to a royalty. It is fully protected under the copyright laws of the United States of America, and of all countries covered by the International Copyright Union (including the Dominion of Canada and the rest of the British Commonwealth), and of all countries covered by the Pan-American Copyright Convention and the Universal Copyright Convention, and all countries with which the United States has reciprocal copyright relations. All rights, including professional, amateur, motion picture, recitation, lecturing, public reading, radio broadcasting, television, video or sound taping, all other forms of mechanical or electronic reproduction, such as information storage and retrieval systems and photocopying and the rights of translation into foreign languages, are strictly reserved. Particular emphasis is laid upon the question of readings, permission for which must be secured from the author's agent in writing. The stage performance rights in *The Mystery of Attraction* (other than first class rights) are controlled exclusively by Dramatists Play Service, Inc., 440 Park Ave. South, New York, NY 10016. No professional or nonprofessional performance of the play (excluding the first class professional performance) may be given without obtaining in advance the written permission of Dramatists Play Service, Inc., and paying the requisite fee. Inquiries concerning all other rights should be addressed to The Gersh Agency, 41 Madison Ave., New York, NY 10010. Attn: John Buzzetti.

THE NINTH CIRCLE by Edward Musto. Copyright 2001 by Edward Musto. Reprinted by permission of the author. All rights reserved. The entire text of *The Ninth Circle* has been published by NY Theatre Experience in the anthology *Plays and Playwrights 2003*.

OTHER PEOPLE by Christopher Shinn. Copyright 2000 by Christopher Shinn. Reprinted by permission of John Buzzetti, The Gersh Agency, 41 Madison Ave., 10th Fl., New York, NY 10010. All rights reserved. The entire text of *Other People* has been published in an acting edition by Dramatists Play Service, 440 Park Ave. S., New York, NY 10016, which controls rights for stage performances. CAUTION: Professionals and amateurs are hereby warned that *Other People* is subject to a royalty. It is fully protected under the copyright laws of the United States of America, and of all countries covered by the International Copyright Union (including the Dominion of Canada and the rest of the British Commonwealth), and of all countries covered by the Pan-American Copyright Convention and the Universal Copyright Convention, and all countries with which the United States has reciprocal copyright relations. All rights, including professional, amateur, mo-

227

228

229